POSTCARD HISTORY SERIES

Lincoln

On the Front Cover: Circus Parade on O Street, c. 1910. This westward view from the corner of Eleventh Street shows large crowds watching a circus parade. A band plays atop the wagon, drawn by 10 white horses, in the foreground. The five-story Little Building at right was constructed in 1907 from designs by Fiske and Dieman. A remodeling in the mid-1930s removed the cornice and added a limestone-clad sixth floor. (Edward Zimmer.)

On the Back Cover: Greetings from Lincoln, Nebraska. The prolific publisher Curt Teich and Company (C.T. & Co.) issued hundreds of thousands of postcards from the 1890s to the 1970s, including many of these "Large Letters" cards made for cities and states. The landmarks featured within the letters of this mid-1930s card include, from left to right, the newly finished Nebraska State Capitol (also shown at lower right), the University of Nebraska's "Ag Campus," Lincoln High School, the Sunken Garden, the Stuart Building (now called University Towers), an aerial view of the University of Nebraska's "City Campus," and Lincoln's U.S. Veterans Hospital. (Edward Zimmer.)

POSTCARD HISTORY SERIES

Lincoln

Edward Zimmer and James McKee

ARCADIA
PUBLISHING

ISBN 978-1-4671-0818-8

Published by Arcadia Publishing
Charleston, South Carolina

Printed in the United States of America

Library of Congress Control Number: 2021951103

For all general information contact Arcadia Publishing at:
Telephone 843-853-2070
Fax 843-853-0044
E-mail sales@arcadiapublishing.com
For customer service and orders:
Toll-Free 1-888-313-2665

Visit us on the Internet at www.arcadiapublishing.com

To our "PALs" at the Preservation Association of Lincoln who share history to build community.

Contents

Acknowledgments

The images for this volume are drawn from the collections of coauthors James McKee (JM) and Edward Zimmer (EZ). We are grateful to our colleague Matthew Hansen, who also collaborated with us on *Lincoln's Early Architecture* (Arcadia Publishing, 2014) for locating some key images. Matt's knowledge of postcard history also enriches the introduction.

INTRODUCTION

Welcome to an incomplete history of Lincoln conveyed through the limited medium of postcards. Since all histories are incomplete and all mediums are limited, a few words of introduction to the city of Lincoln, postcards in general, and this book may add to the reader's understanding and enjoyment.

Lincoln was originally called Lancaster, a tiny town founded in the 1850s beside Salt Creek's saline marshes in the Territory of Nebraska. Only about 30 residents called Lancaster home when it was selected in 1867 to be the capital of the newly admitted state of Nebraska. The U.S. Census of 1870 counted about 2,500 residents; by 1880, about 13,000 resided in Lincoln, and 55,000 were enumerated in the 1890 count. Nationwide economic reversals in the 1890s saw the young city's population drop to 40,000 by 1900, while the new century brought slow but steady growth. The population did not again reach the 1890 total until the mid-1920s. Only with annexations of four suburban towns between 1926 and 1931 did Lincoln exceed 75,000 residents.

Founded as the seat of Nebraska's state government and the location of the state university, prison, and asylum, Lincoln also prospered as a hub of multiple rail lines; an educational, legal, financial, and medical center; and the heart of a fertile agricultural region with associated food processors, farm-implement dealers, and grain brokers.

Postcards have rich potential and clear constraints in the context of displaying a city's history. Perhaps foremost among them is that they barely existed before the 20th century, having originated at the World's Columbian Exposition of 1893 in Chicago and then only as issued by the U.S. Post Office and focused on that fair. "Penny postcard" referred to the typical cost of a card and also its postage. When privately issued cards were authorized a few years later, the postal stamps for them cost twice as much—2¢!

Privately issued picture postcards were allowed for the same penny rate in 1898, but until 1907, only a stamp and address were allowed to be included on the back of a card. A few cards from that early era are presented in this volume, with brief notes squeezed onto the margins of the cards' fronts. A major innovation came in 1907, when divided back cards were authorized; these had the address on half of the reverse side with the remainder reserved for messages. Postcard popularity exploded before World War I, with nearly a billion cards mailed each year in the United States in the early 1910s. Most of the cards in this book are divided back cards that date from 1907 through the 1930s.

Postcards came from multiple sources—businesses promoting products, national or international publishers targeting travelers and students, chambers of commerce "boosting" their locales. Adding some greater diversity to postcard images are real-photo cards. These feature postcard stock preprinted on the reverse of photographic paper, on which amateur or professional photographers could expose their own images. Some of these were mailed; others may never have been intended for postal use, but the images are often crisp, clear, and unique.

There are limitations to viewing local history through the lens of postcards. For Lincoln's history, time frame is one—the city's early years predate postcards, and postcards' heyday was relatively brief, so this book tilts heavily toward the first few decades of the 20th century. Many consequential sectors of the community are poorly represented in postcards. Despite Abigail Adams's sound advice to her husband, John, to "Remember the ladies," they may sometimes appear forgotten in these images. However, they are remembered in the captions. Economically disadvantaged community members—including Black residents and the large immigrant population, especially Germans from Russia—appear in few of these images, although Lincoln's John Johnson, a talented Black photographer, probably produced some of the real-photo postcards. (See *Lincoln in Black and White: 1910–1925*, published by Arcadia Publishing in 2008, for more of his work.)

We sorted through hundreds of postcards before selecting and then organizing the 211 chosen to be part of this book. Chronology and topics did not appear to be useful structures, so geography became our guide, as the chapter headings may hint.

Since Lincoln is Nebraska's capital city, we chose to begin—in chapter one—with Nebraska's capitol buildings, with the second and third capitols especially well represented in postcards.

Because the capitol has been located on the south edge of downtown Lincoln since the city's founding, chapter two considers sites between the capitol and O Street—Lincoln's "main street."

Chapter three focuses on O Street itself from east to west.

Chapter four concerns Haymarket and its environs, a special neighborhood at the west edge of downtown dominated by industrial and warehouse spaces and the rail yard.

Chapter five traverses downtown north of O Street from west to east.

The "City Campus" of the University of Nebraska-Lincoln (UN-L) defines the north edge of downtown, and UN-L's several campuses are considered in chapter six.

Chapter seven encompasses central city sites outside of but close to downtown, moving counterclockwise from southwest to northeast.

Chapters eight and nine address the suburban towns founded on the east edge of Lincoln in the late 1880s and early 1890s.

The concluding chapter ten gathers more dispersed sites, which are ordered in clockwise fashion from near the city's center of Forty-eighth and O Streets and proceed east, south, and southwest to finish at Lincoln Air Force Base.

One

Nebraska State Capitol and Its Neighbors

Gettysburg Lincoln, Installed in 1912. Daniel Chester French sculpted this monumental bronze portrait of Lincoln for the west side of the capitol grounds facing toward J Street (now called Lincoln Mall). The Gettysburg Address is inscribed into the granite backdrop designed by architect Henry Bacon. Bacon and French were the architect and sculptor, respectively, of the Lincoln Memorial in Washington, DC, which was completed in 1915. (EZ.)

NEBRASKA'S SECOND CAPITOL. Because Nebraska's first state capitol was hastily built in 1867–1868 with substandard stone, construction of a replacement became necessary a dozen years later. William H. Willcox was chosen as architect for the second capitol building, which was constructed in thirds, beginning with the west wing, then the east wing. Only then was the old building razed for the completion of the central portion and dome in 1889. (EZ.)

VIEW OF NORTH FRONT, NEBRASKA STATE CAPITOL. A New York publisher issued ornate postcards of the national and state capitols in the early 1900s. The bandstand on the north grounds of the Nebraska State Capitol was dedicated in June 1899 with a concert that opened with Sousa's "The Stars and Stripes Forever" and closed with "The Star-Spangled Banner." (JM.)

NEBRASKA STATE BAND AT THE STATE CAPITOL, C. 1905. The Nebraska State Band was incorporated in 1893 "so that hereafter it might not be deemed advisable to send abroad for high-grade music at state gatherings," according to a Lincoln newspaper. The band posed on the steps of the second capitol for this postcard. (JM.)

THEKLA CARLSON ON THE CAPITOL'S SOUTH GROUNDS, C. 1914. Carlson was a young immigrant from Sweden who worked as a "domestic" (servant), tending the children of a Lincoln household. In this image, Lincoln photographer Gustav Shelander offered a rare glimpse of the lily pond on the south grounds of the capitol but was more focused on portraying Carlson. Carlson and Shelander married in 1915. (EZ.)

Northwest View from the Capitol, 1875. Eight years after Lincoln was founded, a photographer climbed the first state capitol for this view, which was published as a postcard decades later. In the distance at right, the University of Nebraska's University Hall is visible just below the horizon beyond downtown's business blocks. Closer to Capitol Square are houses and vacant lots. (EZ.)

Northwest View from the Capitol, c. 1910. At center is the 32-unit Orlo Flats, built for former mayor A.J. Sawyer in 1907 from designs by Fiske and Dieman. Churches adjacent to the capitol include St. Mary's Catholic Cathedral (the tower at the right edge), First Baptist Church (at right center), and beside it, the smaller Swedish Lutheran (its spire is above Orlo Flats). The steeple of First Baptist points toward St. Paul Methodist Episcopal Church. (EZ.)

CAPITOL SCHOOL. When Lincoln was platted in 1867, five blocks were reserved for elementary schools and one for a high school. Capitol School was built at Sixteenth and F Streets in 1886, then was replaced in 1963 with Clare McPhee Elementary School. That block was originally designated for the high school; instead, Lincoln High School was built in 1871 at Fifteenth and N Streets (and later replaced by Pershing Auditorium). (EZ.)

CAPITOL AREA CHURCHES, C. 1905. Before 1907, postal regulations allowed only addresses on the back of postcards, so any messages had to be written on the front. Holy Trinity Episcopal Church stood two blocks west of the capitol. "New Catholic Cathedral" was built at Fourteenth and K Streets in 1887–1888 as Central Christian Church; a devastating fire during a 1907 remodeling spared only the tower and portions of the outer walls. (JM.)

LINCOLN'S CATHOLIC CATHEDRAL, 1911. Following the 1907 fire, Lincoln's Catholic Diocese rebuilt the Central Christian Church cathedral with a new, simplified roofline and taller secondary tower. The original steeple of the church, built in 1887–1888 from designs by O.C. Placey, was retained, including its "1888" datestone. The rebuilding followed designs by Milwaukee architects E. Brielmaier and Sons. The card's inscription, "St. Theresa's Pro-Cathedral," reflects the name of an earlier Catholic church in downtown Lincoln, whereas the new building was dedicated in 1911 as Cathedral of St. Mary of the Immaculate Conception. This card was sent in 1913 by 17-year-old University of Nebraska student James Laurence Way to "Dear Dad"—Dr. F.E. Way, a prominent physician in Wahoo, Nebraska. The son reported to his father: "Have a typewriter now, an Underwood, certainly a dandy. Have not got a chance to use it much yet, need practice." James served in the U.S. Army's 91st Aero Squadron in France and Germany in World War I, then worked as a civil engineer for the Chicago, Burlington & Quincy Railroad in Lincoln for nearly four decades. (JM.)

SOUTH FACADE OF HOLY TRINITY EPISCOPAL CHURCH. In 1888, the existing Episcopal church on the northeast corner of Twelfth and J Streets was moved to 729 North Twelfth Street, and a new $40,000 stone building with a 120-foot tower and steeple replaced it. The English Gothic–style structure was designed by John Henry Willis Hawkins (1855–1923), a New York–born architect who arrived in Lincoln in 1886 with the advantages of education and experience. Hawkins graduated from Cornell University in 1877, then practiced for nearly a decade in Pennsylvania. He relocated from Lincoln to Omaha in 1890 after five brief but productive years in Lincoln designing churches, commercial and educational buildings, and mansions, including Phillips Castle at Nineteenth and D Streets. Like most of Hawkins's Lincoln projects, Holy Trinity is gone—a fire on January 10, 1957, gutted the church and resulted in the congregation rebuilding out of the city's center at Sixtieth and A Streets. (EZ.)

NEBRASKA'S FIRST GOVERNOR'S MANSION. Until 1899, Nebraska provided no official residence for governors, who instead resided in private homes or hotels. In 1899, the state purchased the D.E. Thompson house, designed by Ferdinand C. Fiske and built in 1892 on the southwest corner of Fifteenth and H Streets. The Colonial Revival mansion was razed in 1956 for the construction of the current governor's residence. (JM.)

THOMPSON FOUNTAIN. D.E. Thompson donated this fountain for the wide Eleventh Street and J Street intersection in 1902. He was general superintendent of the Burlington & Missouri River Railroad, a friend of Pres. William McKinley, founder of the *Lincoln Star*, and an ambassador to Brazil and Mexico. After it was deemed a traffic hazard, the fountain was relocated to Antelope Park around 1920, where the granite ring still encircles a flower bed. The metal figures were eventually scrapped. (EZ.)

Third Nebraska Capitol Viewed from the Southwest. Planning for a third Nebraska State Capitol building began in the 1910s, when the second building faced overcrowding and structural problems. Guided by a well-designed program from Omaha architect Thomas R. Kimball, the Capitol Commission solicited 10 designs and selected the boldest, which was created by Bertram G. Goodhue of New York. Construction began in 1922, and although Goodhue died in 1924, Goodhue Associates completed his design by 1932. (EZ.)

Gettysburg Lincoln, c. 1940. When the third capitol was built between 1922 and 1932, the bronze statue of Abraham Lincoln was the only feature from the second capitol grounds that was retained. It was placed in an enhanced setting with wide granite steps, a flagstone plaza, and low, curved limestone walls. Behind the monumental 9-foot-tall statue of Lincoln, the capitol tower soars to 400 feet tall. (EZ.)

AERIAL VIEW LOOKING NORTHEAST TOWARD DOWNTOWN, C. 1935. This elevated view shows the capitol's lower stories, which contain offices, legislative spaces, and four courtyards. The courtyards bring daylight into internal corridors and offices and were intended to be enhanced with fountains and landscaping; this was finally accomplished in the 2010s. (JM.)

NEBRASKA GOVERNOR'S RESIDENCE. In 1956–1957, Nebraska replaced the original, wood-framed gubernatorial residence at the corner of Fifteenth and H (now Goodhue Boulevard) Streets with a brick home occupying all of the H Street frontage from Fourteenth to Fifteenth Streets. Lincoln architect Selmer Solheim offered the Georgian Revival design after more contemporary alternatives were rejected. Eventually, the entire block was added to the residence's grounds, which are set off by a brick and steel fence. (JM.)

Two

Downtown South of O Street

Lancaster County Courthouse. Lancaster County was formed in 1859. With the 1867 establishment of Lincoln as the state capital, a square block at Tenth and K Streets was designated for a county courthouse. The pictured $170,000 building was designed by Omaha architect F.M. Ellis and constructed from 1887 to 1890 using stone from Berea, Ohio. It was replaced in 1968 with the County-City Building (now the Justice and Law Enforcement Center) on the block immediately south. (JM.)

St. Paul Methodist Church. Lincoln's original 1867 plat offered downtown sites for churches, which 10 congregations accepted. The Methodists built a wooden church at the northwest corner of Twelfth and M Streets in 1868, then constructed a limestone church in 1885, dedicated as St. Paul Methodist Episcopal Church. After the church burned down in 1899, the congregation commissioned Cincinnati architects Brown, Burton, and Davis to design a new brick building in 1901. Denominational mergers in 1939 and 1968 resulted in the more familiar modern name. (EZ.)

Bird's-Eye View of Downtown Lincoln, c. 1910. This view from the belfry of St. Paul Methodist Episcopal Church looks northwest. The ornamental gables of the Herpolsheimer's department store are visible at lower right, with a Rudge and Guenzel sign beyond them. The belfry still stands, housing the McKinley Bells donated by the City of Lincoln, but the original crowning dome and spire were removed in 1912 to alleviate persistent leaks. (JM.)

TWELFTH STREET LOOKING SOUTH FROM O STREET. For this postcard, the photographer's vantage point was atop the six-story Burr Block at Twelfth and O Streets. In the foreground is the Funke Building. Piercing the horizon are St. Paul Methodist Episcopal Church (at left) and the tower of the Lancaster County Courthouse (to the right of center). (JM.)

HERPOLSHEIMER'S DEPARTMENT STORE, TWELFTH AND N STREETS. Just north of St. Paul Methodist Episcopal Church was Lincoln's first department store, Henry Herpolsheimer's "Daylight Store" (as it was nicknamed), built in 1890. It had two stories of huge windows extending along the N Street facade and wrapping the corner. Roberts and Woods designed the eye-catching building with a rounded, turreted corner tower and decorative gables and finials along both street frontages. The store closed in 1930. (JM.)

VIEW LOOKING NORTH ON ELEVENTH STREET FROM M STREET. Lincoln was laid out in 1867 as a grid of regular 300-foot blocks and three "super blocks" for the state capitol grounds, a university campus, and a park. Most streets had 100-foot rights-of-way, but wider 120-foot rights-of-way led to the centers of the super blocks, creating vistas that stitch the city together. Eleventh Street is one such extra-wide street, with University Hall capping the vista. (EZ.)

CHRISTIAN SCIENCE CHURCH, 1201 L STREET. Lincoln's First Church of Christ, Scientist, was designed by Chicago architect Solon Spencer Beman along with a half-dozen Christian Science churches in Chicago. The monumental Lincoln church was built in stages from 1905 to 1912. A cornerstone laid in 1911 was marked "A.D. 1908"—roughly mid-construction. Beman was also the architect of the Bankers' Life Insurance Building at Fourteenth and N Streets in Lincoln. (JM.)

First Continental National Bank, 1201 N Street. The Lincoln architectural firm Davis and Wilson designed this International-style office in 1957 for the Continental National Bank. In 1960, First National Bank of Lincoln (chartered in 1871) merged with Continental National (founded in 1911), resulting in the First Continental name. The lobby housed a 96-foot-long abstract mural, *Riches of Nebraska* by Jimmy Ernst. Additional floors were added to the office building in 1964. (EZ.)

Lincoln Sanitarium/Sulpho-Saline Bathhouse. F.C. Fiske designed this handsome sanitarium, which was built in 1892–1893 on the southeast corner of Fourteenth and M Streets. The facility offered therapeutic baths in the naturally saline groundwater found beneath Lincoln and saltwater swimming in a 40-by-130-foot "plunge" (swimming pool). Two brothers, Drs. M.H. and J.O. Everett, provided medical supervision, and their three physician sons later managed the facility as a hospital until 1928. (EZ.)

TWO SOUTH THIRTEENTH STREET CHURCHES. When Nebraska's Capital Commission laid out the new capital city in 1867, its plan offered free downtown sites for churches. Ten Christian congregations soon built small, wood-framed sanctuaries. As Lincoln's population burgeoned in the 1880s, larger masonry churches replaced most of the wooden buildings. Two congregations built structures in the mid-1880s on the block on the west side of South Thirteenth Street between L and M Streets. At Thirteenth and M Streets, First Presbyterian Church (above) had New York architect Lawrence Valk design a monumental brick church with a very tall, bold tower. Valk's national practice included extant churches in Colorado Springs, Colorado, and Fort Madison, Iowa. At Thirteenth and L Streets, Omaha architect F.M. Ellis designed First Congregational Church (below). Ellis's design was unusual in that the main entrance and steeple were oriented diagonally toward the intersection. (Above, EZ; below, JM.)

CORNHUSKER HOTEL, 309 SOUTH THIRTEENTH STREET. The first Cornhusker Hotel was a 10-story, 300-room facility built in 1925–1926 and designed by Kansas City's Alonzo Gentry. The congregations previously on the block both relocated to nearby sites east of downtown—the Presbyterians to Seventeenth and F Streets and the Congregationalists to Twentieth and D Streets, where they rejoined a sister congregation as First-Plymouth Congregational. The hotel was imploded for the construction of a new Cornhusker Hotel and offices in 1982. (EZ.)

CITY AUDITORIUM. In 1896, Lancaster County acquired the southeast corner of Thirteenth and M Streets for an auditorium. Merchant J.F. Miller and publisher J.C. Seacrest visited Bloomington, Illinois, where Paul Moratz had designed a coliseum. Lincoln quickly engaged Moratz and built using his plans by 1900; the auditorium's curved wooden roof trusses were said to be capable of supporting a locomotive. A 1928 fire destroyed the popular venue. (JM.)

LINDELL HOTEL, C. 1909. The Lindell Hotel stood on the northwest corner of Thirteenth and M Streets directly north of First Presbyterian Church. Dr. A.L. Hoover built the first section of the brick hotel in 1885, replacing a wood-frame hotel previously on the site. Through many additions, the Lindell grew to 200 rooms before it was razed in 1969 for the 20-story office building of First National Bank (later US Bank). (EZ.)

FRATERNITY BUILDING, C. 1910. William E. Sharp and A.O. Faulkner, founders of competing insurance companies, partnered to construct the Fraternity Building on the southeast corner of Thirteenth and N Streets in 1902. James H. Craddock designed the brick and stone office building for Sharp's Royal Highlander Company and other tenants. Additions to the east side in 1904–1905 nearly doubled the size of the original building. In 1926, Sharp replaced the Fraternity Building with the 16-story Sharp Building. (JM.)

SHARP BUILDING, SOUTHEAST CORNER OF THIRTEENTH AND N STREETS. William E. Sharp was still an owner of the quarter-century-old Fraternity Building when he had it demolished in 1926. The next year, Sharp and a new partner, Charles Stuart, constructed the Sharp Building on the site with Joseph McArthur as their architect. McArthur had come to Lincoln from Chicago in 1915 to superintend construction of the Terminal Building for Paul V. Hyland. Sharp's insurance company, the Royal Highlanders, had offices in the new building along with lawyers, dentists, and other commercial tenants. At 16 stories, the Sharp Building remained the tallest private office structure in downtown Lincoln until the 1980 construction of the 20-story First National Bank (later US Bank) Building. The Nebraska State Capitol towers over the city at 400 feet tall but tallies only 13 stories. (EZ.)

Press Building, Thirteenth and N Streets. Lincoln's YMCA constructed its first purpose-built home in 1890–1891 north of the Lindell Hotel. Ferdinand C. Fiske was the architect for the four-story building with a curved corner tower topped with a domed roof. It was called the Press Building for the *Freie Press*, a German-language newspaper published here. In the early 20th century, it had a bowling alley under the Thirteenth Street sidewalk. (JM.)

Interior of Ruppert's Pharmacy, Southwest Corner of Thirteenth and N Streets. In 1935, Woodman Accident and Life Insurance Company replaced the Press Building at Thirteenth and N Streets with an office structure designed by Davis and Wilson. The corner retail space was occupied in the mid-1950s by Ruppert's Pharmacy, which featured locally made sweets such as Baker's Chocolates and Meadow Gold Ice Cream. The 1930s building is extant, but its appearance has been thoroughly remodeled. (EZ.)

RUDGE AND GUENZEL DEPARTMENT STORE. In 1900, Charles Rudge and Carl Guenzel expanded a hardware business into a department store. They constructed a purpose-built store, designed by Berlinghof and Davis with engineer Gilbert Ellsworth, at the northwest corner of Thirteenth and N Streets in 1917–1919 with over 200,000 square feet of space and the latest in fixtures. Acquired by a national chain in 1928, Rudge and Guenzel closed in 1941. (EZ.)

BURROUGH'S CAFÉ, 132 SOUTH THIRTEENTH STREET. Burrough's was a popular downtown café that operated in several locations in the early 20th century. It moved into the storefront of the Nebraska Telephone Building in 1915, advertising "Burrough's Café New Location . . . Serves You Right." The menu for Thanksgiving dinner in 1916 included Wyoming elk. By 1920, the café was operating at 1329 O Street in a similarly ornate storefront. (JM.)

Federal Trust Building. In the late 1920s, three new office buildings on Thirteenth Street bore out the chamber of commerce's boast of "A New Skyline Every Morning." The 12-story Federal Trust Building of 1927 was designed by Lincoln architects Meginnis and Schaumberg for a variety of tenants. Federal Trust has a Gothic cornice of terra-cotta crowning the limestone lower stories. On the block to the north, the 12-story Stuart Building was constructed in 1927, while the 20-story Sharp Building was erected in 1926. Beside the Federal Trust Building, on the lower left side of the postcard, is the diminutive and ornate facade of Woods Bros. Companies Building, constructed in 1916 for several real estate, land development, and construction enterprises that belonged to a leading Lincoln business family. (JM.)

BANKERS' LIFE INSURANCE COMPANY. In early 1910, a Lincoln newspaper reported that "the Bankers' Life building at Fourteenth and N streets will be either a half million [dollar] ten storied office building or a beautiful temple-like structure for the exclusive use of the company." The card shown above reflects the "temple" as designed by Chicago architect Solon Spencer Beman, whose plans for Lincoln's Christian Science church were then in motion. When Bankers' Life began construction late in 1910, the plans included two additional stories for tenants. The insurer moved 220 employees into the new building (shown below) in 1911. This building was demolished after the firm (since renamed Ameritas) relocated to O Street at Cotner Boulevard in the 1950s. To the south (at left, behind the Bankers' Life building) is the small original office of the Lincoln Telephone Company. (Both, EZ.)

LINCOLN CITY LIBRARY. Lincoln's city library was destroyed when its rented quarters in the Masonic Temple at Eleventh and M Streets burned in 1899. Mary Bryan, wife of William Jennings Bryan, contacted Andrew Carnegie, who donated $77,000 for a new library contingent on Lincoln providing ongoing support. The northeast corner of Fourteenth and N Streets was secured, and Lincoln City Library, designed by Omaha architects Fisher and Lawrie, opened in 1902. The Bennett Martin Public Library replaced it 60 years later. (EZ.)

OLD YWCA BUILDING. Lincoln's YWCA organized in 1892 and operated at various locations in its early years. Its first permanent building was constructed in 1908 on N Street near Fifteenth Street, east of the new city library. Fiske and Dieman were the architects of the three-story brick structure. (JM.)

INTERIOR OF LINCOLN YWCA, 1908. The first purpose-built home of Lincoln's YWCA had a handsome Craftsman-style interior with oak woodwork and furnishings. It was replaced by 1932 with the current building at 1430 N Street, a Federal Revival–style, three-story brick building with limestone trim designed by Meginnis and Schaumberg. The YWCA sold the site in 2009. (EZ.)

LINCOLN'S EVOLVING BLOCK 63. Lincoln High School (above) was built in 1871 on one of the six blocks set aside for public schools in Lincoln's 1867 plat. Artemas Roberts and his brother-in-law James Bellangee designed the building located on Fifteenth Street between M and N Streets. An administration building was added to the north (left) in 1897 and linked by a second-story bridge. McKinley Elementary School opened south of the high school in 1902. Decades of legal and financial hurdles stood between the opening of a new Lincoln High School at Twenty-second and J Streets in 1915 and the repurposing of its old site for Pershing Municipal Auditorium (below) in 1956–1957. Four Lincoln firms of "associated architects" designed the auditorium, with Steve Cook serving as superintendent of construction. Pinnacle Bank Arena supplanted Pershing in 2013, prompting its closure in 2014; its demolition (to make way for redevelopment) was pending at the time this book was published (early 2022). (Both, JM.)

Three

O Street, the Heart of Downtown

Rock Island Depot. The Chicago, Rock Island & Pacific Railroad reached Lincoln in 1892 and chose a depot site at Twentieth and O Streets. The brick and stone depot opened to great excitement in May 1893, and a Lincoln newspaper reported that "the handsome and tasty new depot building and the beautiful and well-kept grounds were praised by all." After the railroad declared bankruptcy in the 1970s, the depot became a bank office. (JM.)

Nebraska School of Business, 1519 O St, Lincoln, Neb.

NEBRASKA SCHOOL OF BUSINESS, 1519 O STREET. In 1909, the Nebraska School of Business bought an earlier business college and taught typing, shorthand, bookkeeping, and other office skills. The school's advertisements boasted that Lincoln's demand for skilled office workers exceeded the supply and that "this is a city of schools and culture [and] . . . one of the few large cities free from saloons." The Denney Federal Building parking garage is now on this site. (EZ.)

FROM O STREET TOWARD THE CAPITOL. Originally called Brace Block, the Farmers and Merchants Building at Fifteenth and O Streets framed the view looking south toward the capitol. In 1890, F.C. Fiske designed the five-story building for a site measuring just 142 by 25 feet. Tenants included insurance and banking establishments, and Nebraska Dental School occupied the top story for decades. The building was removed to make way for a parking lot in 1957. (JM.)

ORPHEUM THEATRE, 1500 O STREET. The Kimball Bros. monument works of 1894 was remodeled in 1906, creating this theater below Capitol View Flats. First called the Bijou Theatre, it became the Orpheum in 1909, then the Majestic, Rialto, and—finally—the Varsity. Fifteenth Street did not originally extend north of O Street. Instead, views north from the capitol terminated with the theater and its neighbors until North Fifteenth was opened after 1940 to R Street and the University of Nebraska campus. (JM.)

CHAPIN/ELECTRIC BUILDING, FOURTEENTH AND O STREETS, AND A TENANT. The Chapin brothers employed architects Woods and Cordner for this three-story building that was erected in 1911 for an estimated $45,000. Lincoln Gas and Electric Light Company was an early tenant of what was commonly called the Electric Building. Electric generation in Lincoln began in 1884, when the Lincoln Traction Company produced electricity for trolley cars. Private and public electric utilities competed in Lincoln until Lincoln Electric System brought consolidation in 1971. The Nebraska School of Business, which relocated from 1519 O Street in 1913, was another early tenant of the Electric Building. The school's new location was in a building twice as wide (50 feet) as the old one, and the corner location afforded daylight on two sides, especially in the bookkeeping department classroom at upper left. (Both, JM.)

SOUTHWEST CORNER OF THIRTEENTH AND O STREETS, AUGUST 12, 1908. This postcard shows "Notification Day," when William Jennings Bryan was officially notified of his third (and final) Democratic presidential nomination. The banner to the left of the streetcar bears a portrait of Bryan. An equestrian procession traveled past this corner on its way to the state capitol, where Bryan gave his acceptance speech before a crowd estimated at 25,000. (JM.)

ARMSTRONG CLOTHING COMPANY. Armstrong's started in 1897 near Tenth and O Streets. By 1903, the company had moved two blocks east to the Big Bargain Store, a two-story, 50-foot-wide building at 1217–1221 O Street. The relocation reflected Lincoln's shifting retail epicenter. Even though Armstrong's added a third floor around 1910, its scale was soon outstripped by downtown's leading stores, and Armstrong's was purchased by Ben Simon's clothiers in 1922. (JM.)

MILLER AND PAINE DEPARTMENT STORE, C. 1916. The Miller and Paine store grew tremendously in the 1910s, adding a new two-story anchor building at the corner of Thirteenth and O Streets in 1914 and an eight-story tower west of it in 1916, along with remodeling a five-story addition south across the midblock alley. Berlinghof and Davis designed the handsome brick and terra-cotta complex in the Chicago style that was popular for department stores and office buildings at the time. (JM.)

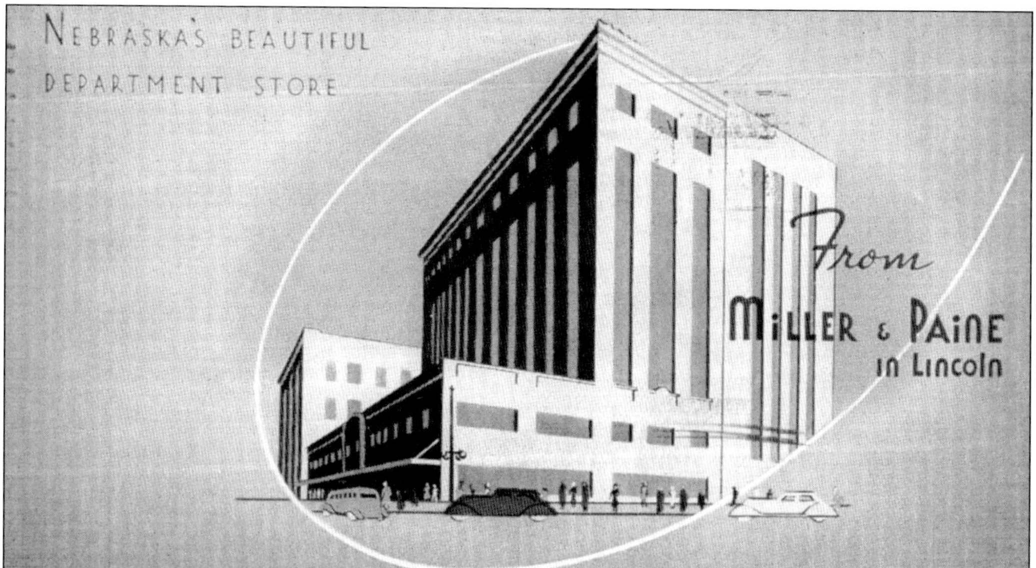

"NEBRASKA'S BEAUTIFUL DEPARTMENT STORE," 1936. Miller and Paine employed Davis and Wilson to design an eight-story addition west along O Street and another five-story building adjacent to the west, both clad in limestone. The additions' sleek, simplified Art Moderne style is exaggerated in this postcard; the 1910s buildings remained unaltered. Miller and Paine built and leased the next structure to the west (not shown on this postcard) to Ben Simon's, a competitor, to solidify the location's retail concentration. (EZ.)

FUNKE BUILDING. The large building at the southwest corner of Twelfth and O Streets was originally the Centennial Opera House, built in 1875–1876. Fred Funke renamed it Funke Opera House and made additions in 1883. James Tyler and Son designed a 1902 remodel, adding offices above the sidewalk-level storefronts. Hallett's jewelry store, a longtime tenant, won a court injunction against disruption during that remodeling. (JM.)

O STREET LOOKING WEST FROM THIRTEENTH STREET. In the early 20th century, downtown's commercial center shifted east along O Street toward Thirteenth Street. The Miller and Paine department store was established at the southwest corner of O and Thirteenth Streets in 1898 and began adding storefronts and stories. This view from about 1910 shows Miller and Paine at left with Armstrong's beside it. On the right, a huge billboard soared above low buildings on the north side of O Street. (EZ.)

BURR BLOCK. This limestone building with a picturesque cornice might be called Lincoln's first skyscraper, as its six-story height was more than double that of most of its neighbors. It even featured one of the city's first elevators. The office building cost an estimated $125,000 to erect in 1887. The architect was James Tyler, and brothers L.C. and C.C. Burr were his clients. The Burrs were leading local promoters, lawyers, and real estate developers; Carlos "C.C." Burr was Lincoln's 12th mayor, serving from 1885 to 1887. The building's roster of tenants was a who's who of Lincoln businesses and professionals—especially lawyers. As a young attorney newly arrived in Lincoln from Illinois in 1887, William Jennings Bryan not only took a partner (A.R. Talbot) and an office at this prestigious address, he also "camped out" in that office until he secured a house where his family could join him. (JM.)

SECURITY MUTUAL LIFE BUILDING, LINCOLN, NEBRASKA

Security Mutual Life Building. Founded in Fremont in 1895, Security Mutual Life Insurance Company was acquired by Lincoln businessmen and moved to Lincoln in 1899. The company purchased the Burr Block in 1906 and had offices in the renamed building by 1908. Perhaps responding to the 1910 construction by First National Bank of an 8-story building (now the Lincoln Building) at Tenth and O Streets, five years later, Security Mutual commissioned architects Berlinghof and Davis to modernize the Burr Block and raise it to 10 stories. Work began on the south half, where workers removed the interior floors, varied windows, and ornate cornice and inserted a new 10-story structural frame within the old stone walls. Completing the redesign were a more uniform window pattern, projecting cornice, and stonework that perfectly matched the original in color and texture. Lessons learned in the laborious south construction led to the north half being razed and rebuilt from the ground up, so only some of the facade stonework on the south half remains in place from the 1887 Burr Block. (EZ.)

"N.E. CORNER 11TH AND O. STREET 1874, LINCOLN, NEB." This card, issued in the early 20th century, shows the north side of O Street in Lincoln's infancy, with wooden stores behind false fronts. By the early 1880s, much of the block had been improved with brick buildings. A fire in 1883 destroyed the corner store. It was replaced by the four-story brick Richards Block, which burned down in 1899. (JM.)

RICHARDS BLOCK, 1100 O STREET. After the earlier building on this corner burned down in 1899, it was replaced with a five-story structure with the same name. A newspaper compared the new Richards Block to the Burr Block "only about 300 feet away," praising the newer building's "meaning and dignity and simple beauty" compared to the "senseless deformity" of the 1887 Burr Block and mentioning that they "are by the same architect." (JM.)

LINCOLN SAFE DEPOSIT VAULT, 126 NORTH ELEVENTH STREET. In 1900, a Lincoln newspaper reported that Lincoln Safe Deposit and Trust Company moved this vault, guarded by "five special policemen," on rollers from the southeast corner of Eleventh and P Streets to a new building immediately north of the Richards Block. The company advertised "private rooms in which to examine papers safely and in secret" behind the doors visible at right. Utilizing the "Fire and Burglar Proof Vault" cost $3 per year. (JM.)

O STREET VIEW. This c. 1910 view shows the south side of O Street east of Eleventh Street. The tall building in the middle of the block housed F.W. Woolworth's Five and Ten Cent Store, the 99th store in Woolworth's chain when it opened in 1904. The crowd may have assembled here for a German Day heritage parade; these were held annually in Lincoln from 1910 to 1913. The parades ceased due to rising international tensions prior to World War I. (JM.)

TWO VIEWS OF THE 1000 BLOCK, SOUTH SIDE OF O STREET. The above scene shows numerous 19th-century structures, including the First National Bank building of 1874 (in the right foreground) on the southeast corner of Tenth and O Streets. Horse-drawn wagons and an automobile parked on the curb beside the bank suggest a date approaching 1910, when the old bank was demolished and replaced by a new office building on the corner. Below, the W.T. Grant store of 1952, the midcentury automobiles, and the large department stores reflect a half-century of change. The Gold's department store began on the corner of Eleventh and O Streets in 1924–1925 and grew through myriad additions. (Above, EZ; below, JM.)

GOLD'S DEPARTMENT STORE BY NIGHT AND DAY. Gold and Company was incorporated in 1915 by William Gold (president) and his son Nathan (vice president). They had Davis and Wilson design a six-story terra-cotta-clad store, which was built in 1924–1925 on the southwest corner of Eleventh and O Streets. The night view (above) shows that original portion. The growing store added four-story wings on the west and south in 1929. Two more stories were added to the west wing in 1947, matching the six-story height of the original corner, while another four-story addition completed the Eleventh Street frontage to N Street. The postcard below dates to after 1947 and reflects the results of each of those building campaigns, all designed by the Davis and Wilson firm. Omaha's Brandeis and Sons bought Gold's in 1964 and closed the Lincoln department store in 1980. (Above, JM; below, EZ.)

VIEW LOOKING EAST ON O STREET FROM TENTH STREET, C. 1910. The foundation under construction in the right foreground is for the 1910 First National Bank Building. Carriages and horse-drawn floats parade eastward, while westbound trolley cars ease past the crowds inbound from their marked destinations: Wyuka "Cemetery" and "21st and Vine." (EZ.)

CLAYTON HOUSE. Lincoln's first bank occupied the northeast corner of the O and Tenth Streets by 1868. After the building was remodeled, it housed the Speier and Simon department store by 1905. A new four-story Speier Store, built in 1926, was later occupied by Sears, then State Farm. Crossroads Motor Hotel was built here in 1960 and soon renamed Clayton House, which existed from 1964 to 1993. The structure's current use as Crossroads House senior housing required thorough remodeling and the removal of the hotel's rooftop pool. (JM.)

FIRST NATIONAL BANK BUILDING. The 1870s quarters of First National Bank were replaced in 1910 with an eight-story Chicago-style office building designed by Hyland and Green of Chicago. Paul V. Hyland had additional significant Lincoln commissions in subsequent years, including the Terminal Building directly west across Tenth Street. The bank building briefly reigned as downtown's tallest private office building until the construction of the Security Mutual Building (in 1915) and the Terminal Building (in 1916), both at 10 stories. The bank lobby occupied the first story with the tall, arched windows. Leading professionals took offices on the upper floors. The basement contained the bank vaults as well as shops that could be accessed by a staircase down from the Tenth Street sidewalk. One of those shops was occupied by cigar makers Richard Herminghaus and Daniel Helwig. Herminghaus's son Ernst became Lincoln's leading landscape architect between World War I and World War II, designing Pioneers Park, the state capitol grounds, and many other community enhancements. When First National Bank left the building in the mid-20th century, it was renamed the Lincoln Building, which now offers condominium residences on the upper floors. (JM.)

TERMINAL BUILDING. After the Lincoln Traction Company consolidated Lincoln's street railways under the leadership of William E. Sharp, he formed a partnership with other leading businessmen, including Charles Stuart and H.E. Sidles, to construct a major office building at the southwest corner of Tenth and O Streets. Construction began in December 1915 and was finished a remarkable nine months later. Paul V. Hyland of Chicago designed the white terra-cotta-clad structure with a bold terra-cotta cornice. Hyland's superintendent for the Terminal Building construction was Joseph McArthur, who relocated to Nebraska and later designed major buildings in Lincoln and Omaha. Lincoln Traction sold electric appliances from Terminal Building, as it was also a utility, generating power for its trolley cars as well as for commercial and residential customers. The building's name reflects its function as the terminal of the streetcar lines. The Lincoln Traction Company's dispatcher occupied a small mezzanine-level office with a bay window above the north canopy from which he could monitor streetcars to the east and west on O Street as well as on North Ninth and Tenth Streets. (JM.)

O STREET LOOKING EAST, C. 1920. Lincoln boasted of "A New Skyline Every Morning" in the 1920s. This view from Ninth Street contrasts the earlier commercial buildings (right foreground) with the new Terminal Building and others. At left, Government Square features greenery, and the former U.S. Courthouse and Post Office displays a city hall sign identifying its new use after its replacement was built to the north. (JM.)

LINCOLN CITY HALL IN FORMER U.S. COURTHOUSE AND POST OFFICE. Construction on Lincoln's limestone federal building began in 1873 with a French Second Empire design from Alfred B. Mullet, who was then the supervising architect of the U.S. Treasury. During construction, Mullet was replaced by William Appleton Potter, who gave the design a more Gothic flavor. The city purchased the building in 1905 and adapted it as city hall in 1907. (JM.)

Looking Southeast over Government Square, c. 1905. This view from the Lincoln Hotel on Ninth Street shows the rear of the new U.S. Courthouse and Post Office, which was located northeast (left) of the 1870s federal building. The new building faced Tenth Street. At its rear was a loading dock for mail wagons and a lawn featuring diagonal walks leading to a fountain, which sat atop an artesian well. (JM.)

Looking Northwest to Government Square, c. 1905. This view northwest across the Tenth and O Streets intersection shows the former courthouse and post office at left and its new replacement at right. The southeast corner of the block in the foreground remained open and is still a tiny park space with a central fountain that emulates the design of the original Government Square fountain. (EZ.)

SNOWY DAY ON GOVERNMENT SQUARE, C. 1910. John Johnson, a talented Black photographer (and a janitor at Lincoln's federal building), often photographed workers and captured moments portraying their activity at Government Square. This scene shows snow cleared away for the mail wagons to access the post office. At center is the State Journal Printing Company building at Ninth and P Streets, and at right is one of the eagle-crowned lamps that were added to Government Square in 1907. (JM.)

VIEW SOUTHEAST ACROSS GOVERNMENT SQUARE, C. 1910. The new (left) and old (right) U.S. Courthouse and Post Office frame the First National Bank Building of 1910 (center) at Tenth and O Streets. At this time, Lincoln's city hall was newly installed in the original courthouse, and the Government Square fountain is visible near its north entrance. Some residents enjoyed the fountain's highly mineralized water as a daily tonic. (JM.)

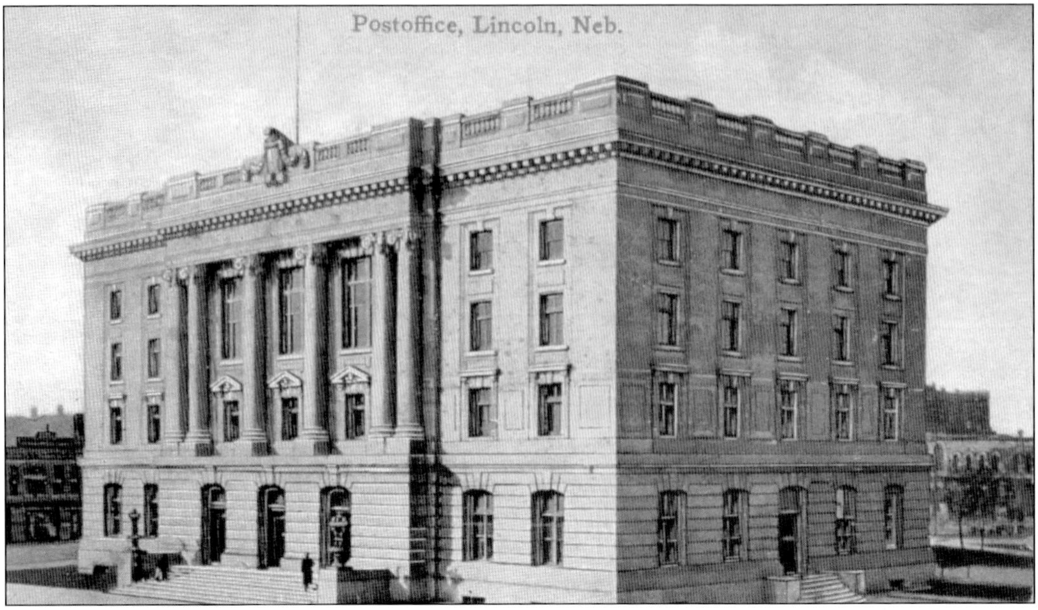

Lincoln's New Federal Building. James Knox Taylor was supervising architect of the U.S. Treasury in 1905 when construction began on a new Beaux Arts–style courthouse and post office on the southwest corner of Tenth and P Streets. Its limestone walls rise from a granite base, and the wide main entrance faces east to Tenth Street. Three tall windows, which light the third-floor courtroom, are flanked by colossal Ionic columns. (JM.)

East Side of North Tenth Street, c. 1905. The new four-story U.S. Courthouse and Post Office provided a perch for photographing this view looking southeast toward Tenth and O Streets. Near the center of the skyline is the dome of the second state capitol. To its right is the belfry and spire of St. Paul Methodist Episcopal Church, and farther to the right is a water tank atop one of the O Street buildings. (JM.)

LINCOLN'S COURTHOUSE AND POST OFFICE EXTENDED. In 1914–1915, less than a decade after construction of the new federal building in Lincoln, a major addition was made to its west side to provide more offices and a much larger mail-sorting room. The materials and overall style of the first wing were closely followed, but some exterior changes and extensive interior remodeling of the 1905 building were carried out. (JM.)

LINCOLN'S COMPLETED COURTHOUSE AND POST OFFICE. In 1939, the westernmost wing of the courthouse and post office was constructed, completing the massive P Street facade that stretches from Ninth Street to Tenth Street. Again, the exterior architecture hewed faithfully to the 1905 and 1914–1915 portions, but on the interior, the three phases of construction were more apparent. Although the original fountain was relocated for each of the first two phases, was eliminated in 1939. (EZ.)

EAST FACADE OF LINCOLN HOTEL FACING GOVERNMENT SQUARE. Omaha architects Mendelssohn, Fisher, and Lawrie designed Lincoln's grandest hotel of the late 19th and early 20th centuries. Construction began on the seven-story Lincoln Hotel at Ninth and P Streets in 1890. It opened the next year with more than 220 fully furnished rooms at a cost of over $400,000. In 1907, Fiske and Dieman designed the south addition, which cost $300,000. (JM.)

HOTEL LINCOLN LOBBY. A succession of owners of the Lincoln Hotel (later the Hotel Lincoln) hosted tourists, business travelers, Nebraska governors (especially before the original governor's mansion was provided), and Pres. William McKinley. Deemed old-fashioned in 1972, the grande dame of Lincoln hotels was demolished for construction of the Lincoln Hilton, which later became the Ramada and Holiday Inn. In 2017, the hotel was rebranded and remodeled as the Graduate Lincoln (JM.)

Four

Haymarket and Environs

Looking East from the O Street Viaduct, c. 1910. Travel on O Street west of downtown was hampered by numerous railroad crossings until 1894, when a viaduct was completed from Eighth Street on the east to Third Street on the west. The iron structure with wooden planking carried a streetcar line and had walkways on each side. This first viaduct was replaced in the 1950s with the Harris Overpass, which rises from Ninth Street. (EZ.)

View of 1908 Salt Creek Flood from Viaduct. A major Salt Creek flood in July 1908 inundated Lincoln's rail yard, West O Street, and the Bottoms neighborhoods. The O Street viaduct descends into the floodwaters in this westward-looking image. The two-story Nebraska Paint and Lead Company building at center features a bridge connecting its upper-floor offices to the viaduct. The houses in the background are in water up to the windowsills. (JM.)

Haskell's Baseball Team, 1909. George Washington Haskell's barbershop was located a few doors south of O Street at 121 South Ninth Street in 1909, when the baseball team he sponsored was photographed on the front steps of his shop. The barbershop had moved to the new Terminal Building by 1918. Art galleries have occupied the Haskell's location pictured here and the adjacent storefronts for over a half century, since the early 1970s. (JM.)

E.E. Bennett Casket Company, c. 1910. The railroad sidings south of O Street served a variety of industries. Edward E. Bennett came to Lincoln in 1886 to establish Wisconsin Furniture and Coffin Company. Rechristened with his own name in 1907, the business grew to fill this five-story, 200-foot-long factory at Sixth and L Streets before moving to Seventeenth and Y Streets in 1917 under a new name: Nebraska Casket Company. (JM.)

Lincoln Drug Company Building. In 1905, Ferdinand C. Fiske (with Charles Dieman of Cedar Rapids, Iowa) designed this blocky warehouse at the southeast corner of Eighth and P Streets for a wholesale druggist. A fifth-story added to the building in 1919 was the work of Fiske and Meginnis. A salesman for the Lincoln Drug Company used this card to schedule a 1909 sales call with a druggist in Norman, Nebraska. (EZ.)

GRAINGER BROTHERS WHOLESALE GROCERY, C. 1910. The five-story warehouse at right was designed by F.C. Fiske and built in 1906; it is extant at 733–737 P Street. The corner building was originally the Tremont House hotel of 1885, which Grainger Brothers converted to offices and a warehouse in 1904. The Salvation Army commissioned Bill Schlaebitz to design a compatible replacement (currently at the southwest corner of Eighth and P Streets) in 1966. (EZ.)

VIEW LOOKING NORTH FROM O STREET VIADUCT, C. 1905. The Burlington & Missouri River Railroad reached Lincoln in 1870—the first rail line to do so. In 1880–1881, Burlington replaced its small frame depot buildings in the rail yard with a brick and stone depot designed by Omaha architect Andrew T. Large Jr. Its footprint between P and Q Streets was originally part of Seventh Street's right-of-way, which shifted east to accommodate the depot. (JM.)

LINCOLN'S BURLINGTON STATION, C. 1905. The Burlington's new Lincoln depot was completed in 1881 at a cost of approximately $55,000. The architecture was called "modern English Gothic" by an 1880 newspaper. Its steep roofs and dormers, arched windows, and sharply contrasting brick and stonework (before soot rendered both of them dark) would now be called High Victorian Gothic. The canopy adjacent to the tracks was added in 1905, then reinstalled beside the new depot of 1927. (EZ.)

BURLINGTON STATION AT 201 NORTH SEVENTH STREET, 1927. The Chicago, Burlington & Quincy Railroad replaced its Lincoln depot in 1927 with a brick and limestone Neoclassical Revival structure by W.T. Krausch of Chicago. It provided travelers' facilities on the ground floor, including a tall waiting room (at center). There are offices on the second and third floors at either end and a single story of offices over the waiting room. (EZ.)

BURLINGTON'S NEBRASKA ZEPHYR, "DAILY BETWEEN CHICAGO, OMAHA AND LINCOLN." The Burlington route pioneered diesel-powered, streamlined passenger trains with the Zephyr in 1934, offering 13-hour service from Chicago to Denver and passing through Omaha and Lincoln. Burlington built several Zephyr train sets for its various passenger routes; the Nebraska Zephyr in the postcard was a 1950s version with a "Fast, Daily Schedule" of 10-hour service between Lincoln and Chicago. (EZ.)

SOUTH FACADE OF CHICAGO & NORTHWESTERN RAILROAD DEPOT. The Missouri Pacific and Chicago & Northwestern Railroads built a "union" passenger station at the northwest corner of Ninth and S Streets in 1897–1898. It was designed in Chicago by the engineering department of Chicago & Northwestern. The handsome brick station with limestone trim and a 100-foot-tall clock tower was demolished in 1953. The southbound terminus of Interstate 180 now descends across this site. (JM.)

Five

Downtown North of O Street

Lincoln's Municipal Building. The block bounded by Q, R, Ninth, and Tenth Streets was dedicated for the library association and historical society in 1867. However, the city instead installed hayscales on Haymarket Square, adding this building in 1886 to house the fire department, police, jail, city clerk, and council chamber. With automated electric horse-stall openers and harness chain droppers, the fire wagons could be ready to go in 17 seconds. (JM.)

Savoy Hotel. The Ledwith Block had offices above shops when it was built at the northwest corner of Eleventh and P Streets in 1887. It was adapted as Merchants Hotel in 1891 but called the Savoy Hotel by 1907. The Savoy's proprietor, Llewellyn Lafayette "Bud" Lindsey, was a Black college graduate who first worked in Lincoln as a waiter, then operated a saloon and cigar store and managed the federal building before acquiring the hotel. Lindsey had two more stories added in 1911, as shown in the below card. Lindsey himself mailed this card in 1916 to a man in Emerson, Nebraska, writing: "You will find the Savoy Hotel a pleasant place to stay while in Lincoln." From 1934 to 1975, it operated as the Sam Lawrence Hotel, which was demolished in 1990. Embassy Suites now occupies this site (and the rest of the block). (Both, EZ.)

LINCOLN COMMERCIAL CLUB. Lincoln Commercial Club was the successor to the Board of Trade and the predecessor of the Lincoln Chamber of Commerce. Formerly housed in the Fraternity Building, the club hired George Berlinghof in 1910 to design its own quarters at Eleventh and P Streets. Berlinghof and new partner Ellery Davis designed a monumental clubhouse with stores on the first floor and second-floor offices, topped by the grand dining/ballroom of the Commercial Club. (Mezzanines constituted a fourth floor.) The above card, a lively perspective rendered by F.W. Fitzpatrick, was probably prepared for fundraising purposes. The real-photo postcard below shows the design faithfully constructed by 1912. Later "remuddlings" removed much of the original character, but gradual renewal efforts in the late 20th century culminated in a thorough restoration of the grand ballroom as an elegant reception space by 2020. (Both, EZ.)

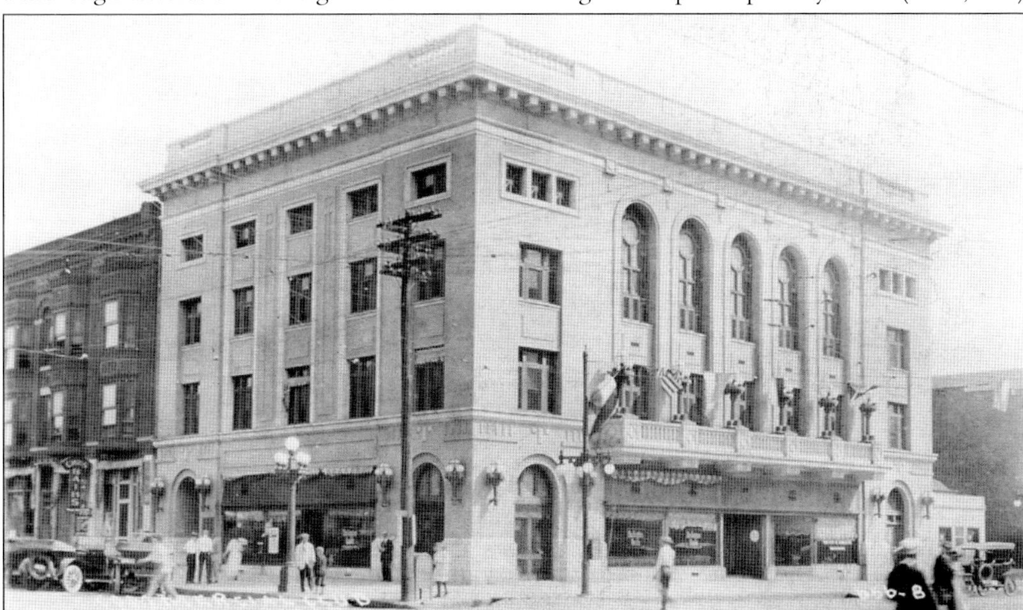

The Hotel Capital. The southwest corner of Eleventh and P Streets was swampy ground until 1869, when a three-story building was constructed there. That building became the Douglas Hotel, which was enlarged as the Commercial Hotel in 1873. A subsequent owner renamed it the Capital Hotel. In 1916, Eugene Eppley razed the earlier structure to build the 10-story hotel pictured here. The tower became Georgian Place condominiums in 1983, with the YMCA serving as the primary tenant of the ground floor until 2021. (JM.)

THE ORPHEUM THEATRE. The Orpheum was built in 1913 on the northwest corner of Twelfth and P Streets. Retail shops and offices surrounded the auditorium. The vaudeville theater had basement dressing rooms and facilities for animals, including elephants. Photoplays (movies) eventually shared the playbill. The Orpheum became the Nebraska by 1939, then was razed to make way for Plaza Theatres in 1972. That building has been repurposed as commercial space and the Arbor Day Foundation's offices. (JM.)

THE GRAND HOTEL. The hotel at the northwest corner of Twelfth and Q Streets opened in 1888. A complete remodeling in 1901 added electricity, bells, and steam heat in all 105 rooms. The University of Nebraska bought the hotel for use as a women's dormitory in 1908. When the university sold it in 1920, it reverted to a hotel. It was closed as a fire hazard and razed in 1960, and the site is now part of Lied Performing Arts Center. (JM.)

The Elks Club. The Benevolent and Protective Order of Elks (BPOE) Lodge No. 80 organized in Lincoln on March 10, 1888, with 65 charter members. After meeting in various rented quarters, the group built its hall on the northwest corner of Thirteenth and P Streets in 1905; it was designed by Tyler and Son. The Elks moved to Fifteenth and P Streets in 1966. This clubhouse was razed in 1971 and replaced by a small movie theater that was later converted to commercial space. (EZ.)

Looking West on P Street from Thirteenth Street, c. 1912. This detailed real-photo postcard shows the Oliver Theatre at left with F.C. Zehrung's townhouse just to its west. The Elks Club is on the north side of P Street, with an auto livery beyond it. The mix of horse-drawn vehicles and gasoline-powered automobiles is characteristic of the 1910s. (EZ.)

OLIVER THEATRE. Postcards often were retouched to advertise a single tenant in a large building. This card featuring the Oliver Theatre is titled "The Home of the Lincoln Business College." The theater was called the Lansing when it opened in 1891, then renamed the Oliver, then Liberty (after World War I), and finally the Varsity. Other tenants surrounding the theater's auditorium included the Lincoln City Library and the University of Nebraska's Dental College. (EZ.)

YMCA. First established as the Young People's Christian Association in 1876, Lincoln's YMCA organized in 1880 with 13 members. Ferdinand Fiske designed the Y's second purpose-built home, constructed in 1909–1911 for $200,000 on the northeast corner of Thirteenth and P Streets. This building was replaced in 1973 by the Douglas 3 theater, which was removed in 2006. The site became Tower Square in 2014, featuring Jun Kaneko's 57-foot glass tower known as *Ascent*. (JM.)

Lyric Theatre. The Lyric Theatre at 132 North Thirteenth Street was designed by James Craddock and built in 1906 by Charles Stuart. It was part of the Acme Amusement Company's Lincoln holdings, which included the Orpheum (later Nebraska), Wonderland, and Majestic Theatres. In 1927, the Lyric Theatre and the Nebraska Buick Company to the north (left) of the Lyric were razed for the 12-story Stuart Building (now called University Towers). (JM.)

Lincoln Hospital (or Ramethenian Restorium). Banker John D. MacFarland's Queen Anne mansion, designed by J.H.W. Hawkins, at the northwest corner of Fourteenth and Q Streets was the "marvel of Lincoln" when it was constructed in 1886–1887 for $50,000. After MacFarland's death in 1902, it became Dr. Ramey and Dr. Carothers's Lincoln Hospital. The mansion was demolished and a Safeway store and gas station were built on the 200 feet of Q Street frontage in 1937. (JM.)

Six

University of Nebraska Campuses

The University of Nebraska. The original campus of the University of Nebraska spanned four square blocks—about 10 acres. It is shown here in a view looking northwest from the intersection of Twelfth and R Streets. The only extant building is the University Library (now Architecture Hall) on the horizon at left. The site with four small houses at lower left is now a corner of the Lied Performing Arts Center complex. (EZ.)

UNIVERSITY HALL. The first University of Nebraska building was University Hall, which sat in the center of the original campus. It was designed by Matthew J. McBird of Logansport, Indiana, and construction began in 1869. The school opened in 1871, but University Hall needed frequent and significant repairs. The mansard roof and upper stories were removed in 1925, but the lower portion continued to be used until it was finally razed in 1948. (JM.)

BIRD'S-EYE VIEW OF LINCOLN FROM UNIVERSITY HALL, C. 1910. This view looking south on Eleventh Street from the University of Nebraska shows how Lincoln had grown in four decades. The three-story building left of center is the hotel first known as the Gorham House in 1885 and later as the Windsor, the Nebraskan, and ultimately the Park-O-Tel. The tower in the background at right is the Lancaster County Courthouse. (EZ.)

NEBRASKA CONSERVATORY OF MUSIC. Willard Kimball was hired for the University of Nebraska's music program in 1893, but a depression ended that initiative almost immediately. Kimball built his own music school across from the campus at Eleventh and R Streets. The private enterprise, called University School of Music, was finally purchased by the university in 1930. The building was later razed, and Kimball Recital Hall opened on the site in 1969. (JM.)

TEMPLE BUILDING. When John D. Rockefeller Jr. offered funding for a student activities building on the university campus, *Omaha World Herald* editorialized that Nebraska did not need his "ill-gotten funds." Undeterred, the regents accepted the gift, and the Temple Building was completed in 1908 adjacent to campus, across R Street. Howell Theatre was added in 1954, and KUON television started in the basement in 1956. More recently, a $5.3 million gift from Johnny Carson funded a thorough renovation. (JM.)

UNIVERSITY LIBRARY. In 1891, Omaha architects Mendelssohn, Fisher, and Lawrie designed the university's first purpose-built library, which was completed in 1895 as the original campus's fifth structure. After Love Library was built in 1945, the old library became Architecture Hall, which was expanded by a link to the old College of Law in 1985–1987. Now the campus's oldest building, the old library retains most of its exterior form and many original interior features. (JM.)

LAW BUILDING. In 1891, the College of Law was formed after the university absorbed a fledgling private law school. The first classes met in University Hall, then found various quarters until the 1913 completion of the College of Law building (pictured), which was designed by Lincoln architects Berlinghof and Davis and located on the southwest corner of City Campus. "Old Law" was linked to Architecture Hall a decade after new quarters for the College of Law opened on East Campus in 1975. (JM.)

CHEMISTRY LABORATORY. When the $69,500 chemistry building on the southeast corner of the university's campus was dedicated in 1885, it was called the most complete and up-to-date chemistry facility west of the Mississippi. It was designed by William H. Willcox, architect of Nebraska's second state capitol. After Avery Laboratory was completed in 1919, the chemistry building became the College of Pharmacy. It was razed in 1958 to make space for the Sheldon Museum of Art. (EZ.)

GRANT MEMORIAL HALL. After Union army veterans advocated for a memorial to Pres. Ulysses S. Grant, one was built in 1887 north of the chemistry building. The drill hall (or the armory) doubled as a gymnasium until the coliseum was finished. A west addition (visible at right) was completed in 1899. The hall became the women's physical education building in 1927, was condemned in 1965, and was razed in 1966. (JM.)

"THE BIG FIGHT" AT NEBRASKA FIELD, TENTH AND T STREETS. Physical disputes between University of Nebraska classes began as early as 1883 with skirmishes over a simple stick designated as a class "badge." In 1905, freshmen kidnapped a sophomore leader for five days. Class Olympics were instituted in 1909 in the hope of quelling violence, but three fractures resulted from sanctioned events in 1910, including two at this "free-for-all" at the old football field. (JM.)

MEMORIAL STADIUM. University of Nebraska track coach Guy Reed described the university's first football field near Tenth and T Streets as "either as hard as pavement or . . . a sea of mud." Farther north, a second Nebraska Field ran east to west. Soldiers Memorial Stadium, completed in 1923 with 32,000 seats, honors Nebraska's veterans. Prof. Hartley Burr Alexander's inscription for the stadium's original southwest corner reads, "Not the victory but the action/Not the goal but the game/In the deed the glory." (EZ.)

City Campus, c. 1940. The University of Nebraska's crowded original campus is centered at the bottom of this aerial view. By 1910, the university was running out of room, and relocating to University Farm at Thirty-third and Holdrege Streets was considered. Instead, a special tax was levied by a statewide vote in 1914 to fund the expansion of the downtown campus to the north and east. Construction of Memorial Stadium and other major structures followed. (EZ.)

Nebraska Union Building. Although a student union had been discussed in the 1920s, the idea died with the Great Depression. As the Depression waned, student leaders found funding in revenue bonds ($400,000) and a Public Works Administration grant ($350,000). Davis and Wilson planned this Virginia brick and Indiana limestone building. The Union opened on the northeast corner of Fourteenth and R Streets in 1938. The bonds were paid off by 1952. (EZ.)

TEACHERS' COLLEGE. In 1908, the university's Department of Pedagogy was formalized as a teachers' college, holding classes in the Temple Building. Expansion of the campus east to Fourteenth Street created new building sites, and in 1919, the new home of the teachers' college was completed near Fourteenth Street. Coolidge and Hodgdon of Boston and Chicago designed the brick and limestone structure, which included Teachers College High School until University High (now Henzlik Hall) was established in 1955. (JM.)

NEBRASKA STATE HISTORICAL SOCIETY HEADQUARTERS. Nebraska's historical society (now called History Nebraska) has had several homes since it was formed in 1878, including the University of Nebraska and the Nebraska State Capitol. Davis and Wilson designed the current headquarters building, which was dedicated in 1953, centered on the north axis of the capitol at Fifteenth and R Streets. (EZ.)

RENDERING FOR PROPOSED NEBRASKA STATE HISTORICAL SOCIETY LIBRARY. George Berlinghof designed this structure intended to be built east of the capitol at Sixteenth and H Streets. The basement was built in 1910, but further state appropriations were not forthcoming, so it was roofed over for storage. With the 1953 completion of the historical society's building on R Street, the basement was filled in and paved for parking. (EZ.)

THE COLISEUM. After the completion of Memorial Stadium, John Selleck, the university's business manager for athletics, turned his attention to a venue for basketball and events such as graduations. The 9,000-seat coliseum was completed in time for the university's graduation on June 5, 1926. Davis and Wilson designed the brick building, which cost $445,000. (JM.)

MUELLER TOWER. Ralph S. Mueller graduated from the university with a degree in electrical engineering in 1898. He invented the alligator clip soon after graduating and grew wealthy thanks to the manufacturing of millions of the spring-loaded, serrated devices that are used for everything from jumper cables to dental office bibs. Chancellor Edgar Burnett maintained a wish list of campus projects, from which Mueller chose a bell tower. A competition was held among the university's advanced architecture students, and George Kuska's design was chosen. Lincoln architects Meginnis and Schaumberg, who employed Kuska, were then engaged to carry the Art Deco concept to construction drawings. The eight-sided tower is 84 feet tall and topped with a stylized corn motif. The sound mechanism consists of amplified chimes, not the multiple octaves of bells and manual controls of a true carillon. The Mueller Tower was dedicated during the 1949 homecoming festivities. (JM.)

MORRILL HALL. Regent Charles H. Morrill financed the University of Nebraska's paleontological fieldwork as early as 1892. He championed a new museum building, especially after the Nebraska State Museum burned down in 1912. Chancellor Samuel Avery combined a gift from Morrill ($100,000) with state funds ($300,000) to make the museum a reality. Designed by Davis and Wilson, the 65,000-square-foot fireproof museum opened in 1927. For over 40 years, it also housed the Nebraska Art Association's gallery. (JM.)

WHITTIER JUNIOR HIGH SCHOOL. Lincoln Public Schools' first facility built as a junior high school opened in 1923, designed by Fiske and Meginnis. The Neoclassic Revival building included a large auditorium, a gymnasium that could be separated by a folding wall into boys' and girls' sections, a shop for manual skills training, and a health office with provisions for "minor" surgeries. The building at 2200 Vine Street is now the University of Nebraska-Lincoln's Prem S. Paul Research Center at Whittier School. (EZ.)

FERRIS WHEEL AT NEBRASKA STATE FAIR, SEPTEMBER 1910. Early Nebraska State Fairs made no mention of midways. There was no Nebraska State Fair in 1898, but the Trans-Mississippi International Exposition in Omaha that year offered nearly 90 acres devoted to what could be described as midway attractions. After the state purchased the Lancaster County Fairgrounds in 1901, midways became an important part of the state fair's attractions. In this image, Grace Ferguson and Katie Robinson are among the well-dressed young ladies waiting to ride on the Ferris wheel at the Nebraska State Fair's Electric Court. The photographer was electrician "Jimmie" Young of Bethany, who married 18-year-old Ferguson in 1911. When the Nebraska State Fair was relocated to Grand Island by act of the Unicameral in 2008, the former fairgrounds in Lincoln became the Nebraska Innovation Campus, a public-private partnership combining University of Nebraska-Lincoln academic programs, business incubators, and athletic facilities. (JM.)

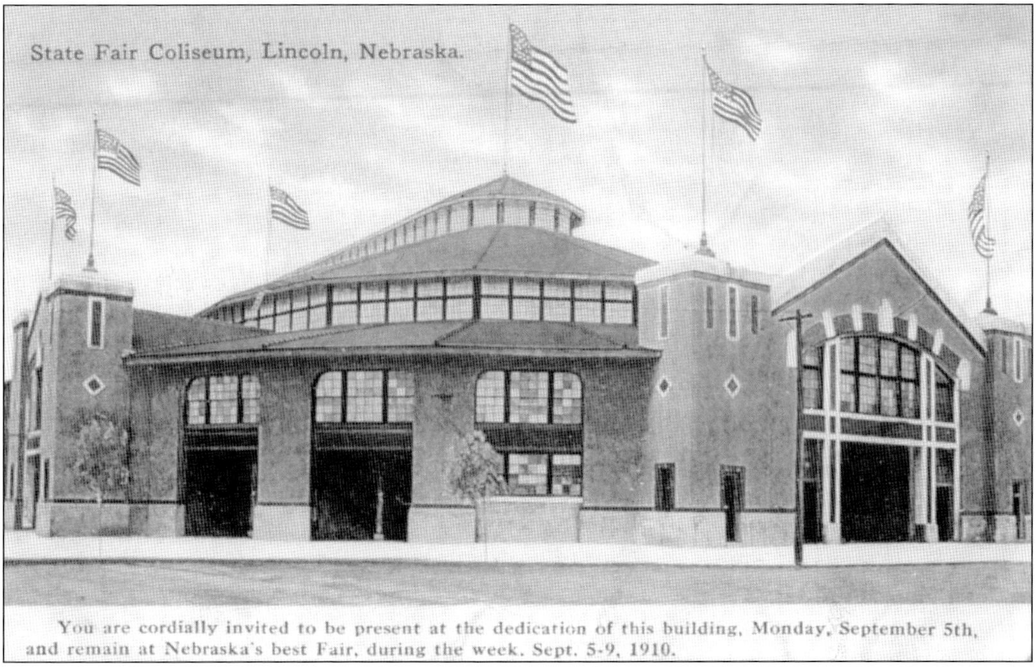

STATE FAIR COLISEUM. In 1909, the Nebraska State Fair sought $115,000 from the legislature to build a massive pavilion for livestock judging. When only $50,000 was appropriated, the optimistic fair board proceeded to have George Berlinghof design a 200-by-350-foot building, then constructed just the southernmost 175 feet. Built of red paving bricks, red tile roofs, and steel trusses over the arena floor, the coliseum had 1,600 seats when it was dedicated in 1910. (EZ.)

FLYING MACHINE OVER LINCOLN. After the Wright brothers' pioneering 12-second flight at Kitty Hawk, North Carolina, in 1903, airplane demonstrations became common at fairs. The Nebraska State Fair featured its first flight (and crash) by a Wright machine in 1910. The fair's 1911 exhibition was advertised with a photograph of that crumpled biplane. In 1912, the fair contracted with John Moisant's International Aviators to fly the French-designed Bleriot monoplane shown here. (JM.)

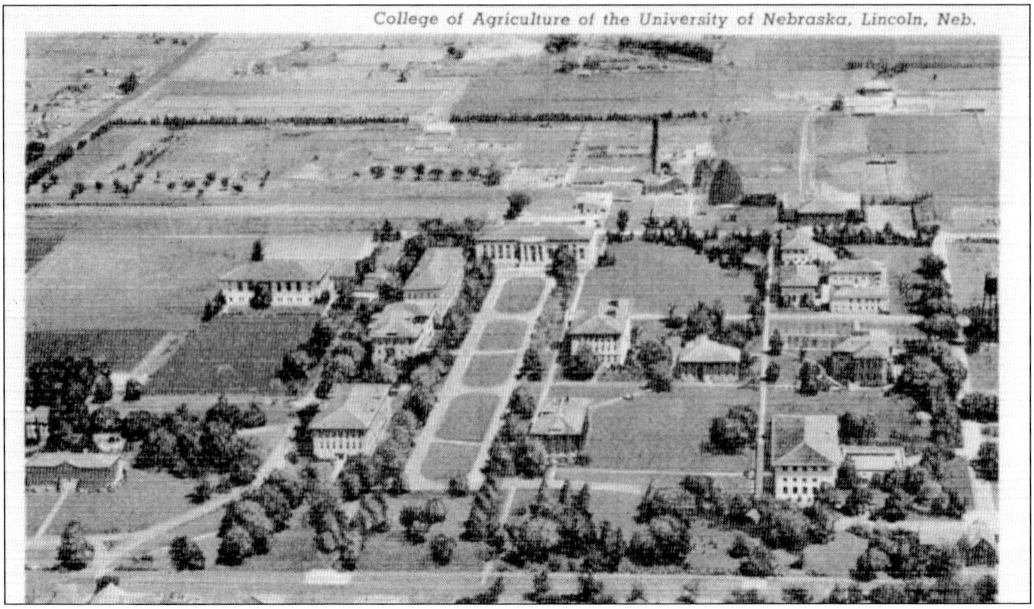

Aerial View of East Campus, 1930s. The University of Nebraska's founding in 1869 under the Morrill (Land Grant) Act required the establishment of a college of agriculture. Toward that end, the university purchased the 320-acre Moses Culver farm on Holdrege Street in 1874 for $17,600. Major College of Agriculture buildings shown in this view still stand and now share East Campus with the College of Law, Dental College, and many other programs. (JM.)

Buildings of the University of Nebraska Farm. This card, mailed between schoolteachers in 1913, shows 4 of the 10 buildings then on the university farm. Only the central one, called the Agricultural Experiment Station, still stands. Designed by Roberts and Woods and built in 1899, it anchors the southeast corner of what is now called the East Campus Mall. That handsome boulevard is shown at upper right ("Park Scene"). (JM.)

Seven

Central Neighborhoods

Robber's Cave. The extensive sandstone cave west of Tenth and High Streets was mostly hand-dug around 1870 by the short-lived Pioneer Brewery for use as a place to cool and store beer. The cave has long generated rumors and legends: Was it used for Pawnee gatherings, a stop for Coxey's Army, or Jesse James's hideout? Around 1906, the cave became a recreation venue; it is now listed in the National Register of Historic Places and open for tours. (JM.)

THE COUNTRY CLUB OF LINCOLN. All three members of Nebraska's Capital Commission (which selected Lincoln as the capital) had Chicago architect John Keyes Winchell design similar mansions for them in 1867. Secretary of State Thomas P. Kennard and state auditor John Gillespie chose sites immediately southeast of the capitol, while Gov. David Butler built this house a mile southwest at Seventh and Washington Streets. After Butler was impeached, his estate had other owner-residents until 1903. It was then leased by the Country Club of Lincoln, which added "a Porch of Mammoth Dimensions" (20 feet by 80 feet) in 1906. When the Country Club of Lincoln relocated to South Twenty-fourth Street in 1923, the old golf course was platted into house lots. The former clubhouse, which stood until 1950, had varied uses, including an Earl May store, a radio station, and Lincoln's Ku Klux Klan lodge in the late 1920s. (Both, EZ.)

ST. ELIZABETH HOSPITAL AND ST. FRANCIS CHAPEL. The Poor Sisters of St. Francis acquired the Buckstaff house at Twelfth and South Streets for $20,000 in 1889 to adapt as Lincoln's first general hospital. St. Elizabeth Hospital grew almost continually with additions of wings and floors. James Tyler and Son designed the first 170 feet of frontage on South Street in 1901. Jacob Nachtigal of Omaha designed the chapel wing added to the south side in 1921. The hospital relocated to South Seventieth Street in 1969, with the old building repurposed as a nursing home. When its demolition was proposed in the mid-1980s, citizens advocated successfully for retention of the chapel wing with its 25 stained-glass windows and traditional ecclesiastic interior. Sinclair Hille Architects designed a new facade in 1994, funded with $250,000 provided by Lancaster County from taxes on legalized gambling. St. Francis Church now functions under the auspices of the Priestly Fraternity of St. Peter. (Above, JM; below, EZ.)

Pioneer Woman. In 1935, the Lincoln Woman's Club financed Ellis Luis Burman's cast-concrete statue, which was installed in a memorial garden on South Thirty-third Street. The club had earlier sponsored Memorial Drive in 1925, which originally extended from Auld Pavilion to Sheridan Boulevard and was marked with an avenue of trees and plantings honoring Lincoln soldiers and Army nurses who died in World War I. (EZ.)

Auld Pavilion in Antelope Park. Banker W.T. Auld purchased the Perkins Tract and an adjacent strip, giving the land to the city of Lincoln in 1915 as an annex to Antelope Park. Auld's gift was noted as "the biggest gift ever made to the city" up to that time. The city memorialized Auld with the naming of the park's pavilion, designed by Berlinghof and Davis and built in 1916. Auld Pavilion originally featured rooftop dances each summer. (JM.)

War Memorial. Like *The Smoke Signal* in Pioneers Park, *Pioneer Woman*, and *Rebecca at the Well* in Sunken Garden, the *War Memorial* west of Auld Pavilion was designed by Ellis Luis Burman. It was funded in 1936 by the Federal Art Project of the Works Progress Administration. The 23-foot cast marble shaft is crowned with a contemplative figure of Victory and surrounded at the base by soldiers of the Revolutionary, Civil, Spanish-American, and First World Wars. (JM.)

ALBERTA AND GEORGE DAVIS HOUSE, 1909. Real-photo postcards were often snapshots of daily life, sometimes taken by amateur photographers and printed on ready-made postcard stock. This view of a nearly finished house at 1745 South Twenty-sixth Street in Lincoln was sent by Voyce Robinson, a young carpenter, to his mother in Tekamah, Nebraska, showing "one of the houses we are building." (EZ.)

PRESCOTT ELEMENTARY SCHOOL. Lincoln architects F.C. Fiske and Harry Meginnis designed this landmark school, which was built at South Twentieth and Harwood Streets in 1920–1922 for an estimated $360,000. It replaced an earlier, smaller 1889 school that stood a few blocks to the north. The school is named for William Hickling Prescott, a prominent 19th-century historian whose grandfather commanded the colonial forces at the Battle of Bunker Hill. (EZ.)

DIERKS-HEMPLE HOUSE, 2144 WASHINGTON STREET. The Dierks family had this large American Foursquare built in 1905. Lumberman Peter Dierks was only 39 years old when he died of typhoid fever in 1906. His widow, LaDesha, raised two children here and made good use of the wraparound porch for "porch parties," entertaining 150 guests at one such party in 1910. LaDesha remarried in 1911 and resided in the house until 1917. (EZ.)

"PRETTY RESIDENCE SECTION." Irish immigrant John Fitzgerald built a mansion in 1880 on a 14-acre estate bounded by today's A, D, Nineteenth, and Twentieth Streets. Fitzgerald's widow sold the property in 1904, and it was subdivided into 55 house lots as the Mount Emerald Addition. Four postcards from the early 1910s celebrated the rapid development of the area, including this one looking east from the corner of Nineteenth and A Streets. (EZ.)

TRINITY METHODIST EPISCOPAL CHURCH. The church complex at Sixteenth and A Streets anchors the south end of the vista along Goodhue Boulevard to the capitol. Trinity's oldest, northernmost portion is a brick chapel with a wide clipped-gable roof; this was designed by F.C. Fiske and built in 1893. Its placement reserved the corner for a gray concrete brick tower and main sanctuary designed by Cleveland architects Badgley and Nichlas and added in 1910–1911. (EZ.)

LOOKING NORTH ON FIFTEENTH STREET. As early as the 1910s, Fifteenth Street between H and A Streets was the first of the capitol's axial streets to receive the special treatment of medians. When the third capitol was completed in 1932, Lincoln landscape architect Ernst Herminghaus prepared planting plans for the Capitol Square and the Fifteenth Street medians. This portion of South Fifteenth Street has been renamed Goodhue Boulevard in honor of capitol architect Bertram G. Goodhue. (EZ.)

I.F. Searle Carriage House and Cars, 1740 C Street. Searle's property included a carriage house in the northwest corner with an apartment for the chauffeur above bays for three cars. The vehicle in the foreground appears to be a Detroit Electric from the mid-1910s, a model said to have been preferred by some female drivers because of its greater ease of operation compared to internal combustion cars, which had to be started by cranking. (EZ.)

Searle House Patio, c. 1915. Lumberman I.F. Searle of 1740 C Street undertook a major project around 1914, removing the adjacent house at the corner of Eighteenth and C Streets and replacing it with a lovely yard with a pergola, lily ponds, and fine outdoor furniture. He hired photographer Gustav Shelander to record his project. Shelander also included the Searles' nanny, Swedish-born Thekla Carlson, whom he married in 1915. (EZ.)

Emma and Jasper Kellogg House. This real-photo postcard shows the Kellogg House, which was built around 1900 and still stands at 1844 D Street. The house is now much altered, having lost its generous porches, which both wrapped around the corner and extended as a drive-through carriage porch at left. (JM.)

Clark-Leonard House. John R. Clark, president of First National Bank of Lincoln, built the city's grandest Queen Anne–style home in 1887 at the southwest corner of Twentieth and F Streets. Englishman James Tyler was his architect. Clark died of a heart attack on his front porch in 1890. In 1905, the house was sold to financier William M. Leonard, whose many remodelings included transforming the west porch into a sunroom. (JM.)

FIRST-PLYMOUTH CONGREGATIONAL CHURCH, TWENTIETH AND D STREETS. In the late 1920s, First Congregational Church sold its downtown site at Thirteenth and M Streets for construction of the Cornhusker Hotel and merged with Plymouth Congregational at Seventeenth and A Streets. The united congregation built a new hilltop church at Twentieth and D Streets between 1929 and 1931; it was designed by H. Van Buren Magonigle and Robert McLaughlin Jr. of New York City. The church's building committee rejected Colonial and Gothic Revival proposals by other architects, praising the chosen design as "original," "independent," and a "new type of church architecture." In the words of the architects, the mixed palette of bricks included "the true colors of Nebraska, the rose for the sunset, the gold for harvest fields." The 171-foot-tall, 16-sided tower with a full carillon is First-Plymouth Congregational Church's most prominent feature, with sculptures of the Four Evangelists crowning the corner piers. (JM.)

LINCOLN HIGH SCHOOL, 1915. The parents of Lincoln High students voted to put the city's new high school on the 16-acre Davenport Tract at Twenty-second and J Streets. Berlinghof and Davis designed the handsome Neoclassical Revival building, which was the first in the city constructed of reinforced concrete. The classes of 1909 and 1911 donated the cornerstone, which was laid in 1913. The still-incomplete building opened on September 14, 1915. (EZ.)

ELLIOTT ELEMENTARY SCHOOL. The imposing west facade of this Fiske and Meginnis–designed school, facing Antelope Creek, is grander than the main Twenty-fifth Street entrance. This taller facade was highly visible from Lincoln High, downtown Lincoln, and the capitol. This school replaced an 1888 building at Twenty-sixth and O Streets and was named for Phebe Elliott during her tenure as the first woman to serve on the Lincoln Board of Education. (EZ.)

MUNICIPAL SWIMMING POOL. "Muny Pool" opened in 1921 to boasts in the newspaper that Lincoln's 100-by-210-foot pool was the "Largest Artificial Swimming Place in State." The north end had a "zero-depth" entry, with about four feet of depth at the south edge and 10 feet at the center. Originally, the pool offered ice-skating in the winter. From 1947 to 1954, the merged Circlet and Lincoln Community Theatre operated from the bathhouse, which is the only pool feature still extant. (JM.)

WICKERSHAM-SMITH HOUSE, 2701 O STREET. This large house was built in 1888 for the family of Charles Wickersham, a train dispatcher. Coal dealer George I. Smith and his family probably added the porches in the early 20th century. A Safeway grocery store replaced the house in 1930 at what became a commercial intersection. The Safeway was succeeded by a furniture store, drugstore, and many other businesses. (JM.)

THE COUNTRY GENTLEMAN RESTAURANT. This restaurant at 2420 O Street opened in 1949. Etta Bauer, an early proprietor, was a sister of Raymond Bauer, whose House of Bauer candy company was next door at 2440 O Street. In the 1960 and 1970s, Etta's partner Cecil Cooper called the café Cooper's Restaurant and Drive-In. Mid-Town Motel occupied the back of the property. More recently, the site housed an Asian American grocery. (JM.)

NORTHEAST BRANCH LIBRARY. George Berlinghof designed the Carnegie-funded library at Twenty-seventh and Orchard Streets, which opened in 1909. It replaced a library operating out of a grocery store. A decade after the library closed in 1982, the building was moved to 2121 North Twenty-seventh and is now a small portion of the Matt Talbot Kitchen and Outreach agency, which aims to feed and give hope to the working poor, homeless, and hungry. (JM.)

HARTLEY ELEMENTARY SCHOOL. Fiske and Meginnis designed the brick schoolhouse that opened in 1921 at Thirty-third and Vine Streets; it is the oldest extant Lincoln public school of the half-dozen those partners designed. The original building has been extended to the north and south. It is named for Ellis Taylor Hartley, Lincoln's school superintendent in the booming 1880s, who returned as a board member in the economic hard times of the mid-1890s. (EZ.)

ENTRANCE TO WYUKA CEMETERY. In 1869, Nebraska's legislature established Lincoln State Cemetery on flood-prone land west of Lincoln. The appointed trustees rejected that site and purchased 80 acres east of the capital city, naming the site Wyuka for an earlier cemetery in Nebraska City. Surveyor Augustus Harvey, who also laid out Lincoln's original plat, drew the cemetery's curving drives. This is the 1912 entrance with the caretaker's home at left. (JM.)

JOHN M. THAYER MONUMENT, WYUKA CEMETERY. John Milton Thayer arrived in Nebraska from Massachusetts in 1854, serving in the militia and the territorial legislature in 1860. He led the First Nebraska Regiment in the Civil War, rising from colonel to major general. In 1866, he was a member of the Nebraska Constitutional Convention, then one of the new state's first U.S. senators. He was appointed territorial governor of Wyoming and twice elected governor of Nebraska. After his death in 1906, Thayer was buried in Wyuka Cemetery in the Grand Army of the Republic section under a monument bearing his portrait in bronze and the inscription "Erected by a Grateful State." (JM.)

Eight

North around Town

Havelock's Rock Island Depot. Rock Island was the last major railroad to reach Lincoln. In 1892, the tracks from Omaha reached Havelock with a small passenger depot and business siding constructed on the north side of the tracks about a block east of Touzalin. The last Rock Island train ran in 1980. The east–west right-of-way paralleling Seward Street in Havelock became the David Murdoch Trail. (JM.)

HAVELOCK'S "MAIN STREET." The store at left housed one of Havelock's first businesses and its post office in 1890. The village's second post office occupied the tallest masonry building (near mid-view), located on the north side of the street that was first named Jackson, then Pacific, O, and finally Havelock Avenue after Havelock was annexed into Lincoln in 1930. The second post office building, doubled after 1911, is the only extant structure in this view. (JM.)

LANCASTER BLOCK ON JACKSON AVENUE. The Lancaster Land Company, the original developers of Havelock, built this double store around 1890. It is at 6201–6205 Havelock Avenue. Grocery stores were among the principal occupants of the storefronts. The upper floor held the Labor Temple, which is where Burlington Railroad shop workers met in 1922 and planned their part in the walkout that involved 3,593 men in Nebraska and nearly 400,000 railroad workers nationwide. (JM.)

INDIANA AVENUE LOOKING WEST. In 1887, Albert E. Touzalin and others platted 1,920 acres northeast of Lincoln as Havelock, dedicating 300 acres for the Burlington Railroad's repair facility. By 1900, Havelock had 1,480 residents living on residential streets such as this one, which was first named Harrison, then N, Indiana, and Ballard Avenue. C.F. Ballard was Burlington's physician and Havelock's first mayor. His home stands on the northeast corner of Sixty-second Street and Ballard Avenue. (JM.)

HAVELOCK CARNEGIE LIBRARY. In 1906, Andrew Carnegie granted $6,000 to Havelock's library board. The resulting library, designed by Tyler and Son, opened in 1907 facing the public park now at Sixty-third Street and Ballard Avenue. Eventually, Carnegie supported the construction of two libraries in Lincoln and three in University Place, College View, and Havelock, all towns subsequently annexed into Lincoln. The Havelock library was demolished after the construction of the Anderson Branch Library in 1971. (JM.)

BURLINGTON SHOPS AT HAVELOCK. In 1887, the Lincoln Land Company deeded 300 acres of land to the Burlington & Missouri River Railroad with the stipulation that it build a repair shop to replace its Plattsmouth facility. The two-story double-brick building shown here opened on June 13, 1892. Though its early functions of repairing and sometimes building locomotives have changed, nearly all of the shops' structures—much renovated—are still in use today. (JM.)

HAVELOCK GALA DAY, 1908. Gala Day was a community-wide celebration—the Burlington shops closed, merchants had special sales, and attendees enjoyed food, music, and contests such as a tug-of-war between shop workers and merchants. In this image, a cable stretches from the roof of the Holliet House hotel to a landing point at lower left. A white-clad daredevil (left of center) is "flying" down the cable hanging only by his or her teeth. (JM.)

HAVELOCK SHOPS STRIKE. After World War I, federally nationalized railroads were returned to private control. When the Railroad Labor Board, which Pres. Woodrow Wilson created to address labor issues, reduced wages by 12 percent, strikes were threatened nationwide. With demands for wage restoration unmet, nearly 1,000 Havelock workers went on strike on July 1, 1922. This postcard shows workmen marching to the Labor Temple to organize pickets. Eventually, the strike was broken, leaving Havelock's economy devastated. (JM.)

BETHANY TROLLEY. This image from August 24, 1912, heralds the initial run of the second streetcar line linking Bethany with Lincoln. By connecting with the Lincoln Traction Company's State Farm trolley, the new line competed with the Omaha, Lincoln & Beatrice (OLB) Railroad's service to North Bethany. In response, the OLB was forced to lower its rates from eight rides for 50¢ to 5¢ per trip. (JM.)

COTNER UNIVERSITY IN BETHANY, NEBRASKA. Nebraska Christian University opened in 1889 in the village of Bethany Heights east of Lincoln. The school was renamed Cotner University (later Cotner College) when Samuel Cotner of Omaha donated a large tract of land during one of the school's several funding crises. (JM.)

COTNER UNIVERSITY'S "OLD MAIN" BUILDING. The Cotner campus extended from today's Cotner Boulevard (west) to Colby Street (north), North Sixty-eighth Street (east), and Alyesworth Avenue (south). The only other building on campus was a gymnasium. The school closed in 1933, although this building, designed by Otis H. Placey, stood until 1951. The former campus was subdivided and developed with residences and the Bethany Branch Library. (EZ.)

NEBRASKA WESLEYAN UNIVERSITY. In 1886, 24 men met at Lincoln's St. Paul Methodist Episcopal Church and agreed to consolidate Nebraska's three Methodist colleges into one school near Lincoln. Gibbs and Parker of Kansas City designed the building, which was dedicated on October 24, 1888, on a 44-acre campus. Tuition was $40 per term. The surrounding community—University Place—incorporated in 1889. Wesleyan's Old Main is the only extant original structure of any Lincoln-area college. (JM.)

FIRST METHODIST EPISCOPAL CHURCH. For 13 years after the 1886 formation of Nebraska Wesleyan University, University Place Methodists met for services in Old Main's chapel. In 1900, lots were acquired west of campus for a church designed by architect (and former Wesleyan instructor) A.W. Woods. Services commenced in the basement in 1903. The sanctuary, which was not completed until 1909, features a 1,000-square-foot art-glass domed ceiling with Abraham Lincoln's face at its center. (EZ.)

WARREN AVENUE. University Place was sometimes described as the "Holy City nigh unto Bethany." Its main street was suitably named for Methodist bishop H.W. Warren. Warren Avenue became North Forty-eighth after University Place's 1926 annexation to Lincoln, when the suburb's population reached 5,450. This postcard looks south on Warren Avenue toward St. Paul Avenue. First National Bank of University Place is on the right with Dr. William's office upstairs. (JM.)

UNIVERSITY PLACE TROLLEY. The message on the back of this postcard notes that it shows "the first streetcar by our house, 1846 North 27th." Lincoln Traction Company provided service between downtown Lincoln and University Place, the largest of the capital city's suburban neighbors, beginning in the 1890s. The passengers are well-dressed in celebration of the inaugural event. (JM.)

Nine

South around Town

Tabitha Orphanage and Rest Home. When Rev. Henry Heiner's daughter Tabitha died of scarlet fever in 1893, he set in motion plans for a home for the elderly and orphans on 15 acres he purchased at Forty-sixth and Randolph Streets. Named in his daughter's honor, the first three-story building also housed a hospital for a time. Additional land was acquired as the campus grew, and it is now called the Tabitha Nursing and Rehabilitation Center. (JM.)

FAIRVIEW. In 1890, William Jennings Bryan bought five hilltop acres of farmland east of Lincoln for $1,250. A dozen years later, he hired Artemas Roberts to design Fairview, a 25-room mansion built in the Queen Anne style. It was completed in 1902 for $20,000. Fairview still stands with its porch enclosed, its entrance moved to the south, and Bryan Memorial Hospital (now Bryan Medical Center East) buildings framing it on three sides. (JM.)

THE LIONS AT FAIRVIEW. Early in his residency at Fairview, William Jennings Bryan purchased a pair of what he described as Korean lions, although he bought them in Japan. He installed them flanking the steps to his home and called one (with a roaring mouth) "Radicalism" and the other (with sealed lips) "Conservatism." He noted that the "truth lies between." Bryan often greeted visitors and spoke to crowds while standing between these lions. (EZ.)

William Jennings Bryan on the Porch at Fairview. Shortly after Fairview was completed in 1902, Bryan had its windswept southwest porch enclosed for greater comfort. It was on this porch in June 1908 that he waited with friends and reporters for confirmation of his third Democratic nomination for president. As in the campaigns of 1896 and 1900, Bryan was defeated in the general election. But his focus shifted from practicing law to public speaking, and he reportedly became the "highest paid speaker in the world," sometimes giving more than a dozen speeches daily. Because his era preceded radio or even electric amplification, he arguably spoke person-to-person to more individuals than anyone in history. (JM.)

BRYAN MEMORIAL HOSPITAL. William Jennings Bryan donated his house and 10 acres to the Methodists for the construction of Fairview Hospital. After his death in 1924, Bryan's family agreed to renaming it Bryan Memorial Hospital, which opened in 1926. Bryan's residence served as the nurses' residence. Expansion began in 1930 and has never ceased. This postcard shows the original hospital building facing east, with two early additions to the north. (JM.)

GREEN GABLES. When Lincoln Normal University's main building burned down in 1898, Dr. Benjamin F. Bailey purchased the boys' dormitory and 25 acres of the campus in the suburb of Normal. He repurposed the dormitory as Green Gables Sanitorium. In 1958, the Benedictine Sisters purchased the Bailey property for use as Madonna House for long-term elderly care. Madonna Rehabilitation Hospital has evolved and grown into a leading full-service rehabilitation center at Fifty-fourth and South Streets. (JM.)

College View Streetcar. Union College opened in College View, Nebraska, in 1891, and with its inception came the first streetcar line connecting it with Lincoln. Later, that initial service was replaced by the Woods Brothers' so-called highline, which ran down Sheridan Boulevard to College View after 1909. The location shown on this card became Forty-eighth and Prescott Streets when College View was annexed to Lincoln in 1931. (JM.)

Union College University Hall. The Seventh-day Adventist college in College View started ambitiously, erecting four buildings designed by William Conqueror Sisley in 1891. At the center stood University Hall, which included classrooms, offices, a library, and a chapel. None of those 1890s buildings still stand, though the college utilizes handsome buildings from nearly every decade since, including the former Carnegie Library of College View. (JM.)

LADIES' DORMITORY. Union College opened with separate men's and women's dormitories flanking University Hall. The ladies' dormitory, or South Hall, had a tall basement story. The overall L-shaped plan was anchored by a four-story pavilion at the southwest corner with a steep hipped roof from which three-story wings extended north and east. A one-story kitchen infilled the northeast corner of the plan. (JM.)

NORTH HALL. North Hall was originally Union College's men's dormitory. When the school's attendance plummeted following the Panic of 1893, part of the building was leased to the Nebraska Sanitarium in 1896 and later sold to the hospital. When the school recovered and grew, the sanitarium shrank, and North Hall again became Union College's largest dormitory in 1921. This real-photo postcard shows the building after it returned to dormitory use. (EZ.)

L Street, College View. Both of these views look south on L Street, which was renamed South Forty-eighth after College View was annexed to Lincoln in 1931. The cross street was Eleventh Street (now Prescott). The city band shell at the terminus of the streetcar tracks was later moved east out of the street right-of-way. Trolley-riders from Lincoln visited the shady campus on hot summer Sundays, when businesses were open in the Adventist town and boys sold "peanuts and soda pop" to the visitors. Many Adventists espoused vegetarianism and promoted peanuts as a protein source. A.W. Herrick, whose general store is visible at right in both views, also sold real estate with advertisements in 1909 highlighting "Peanut Hill," the suburb's nickname. College View's David Weiss manufactured peanut butter for years, supplying Lincoln grocers as well as his Peanut Hill neighbors. (Both, JM.)

COLLEGE VIEW STREETSCAPE. This view shows Eleventh Street (now Prescott) looking west across L Street (now South Forty-eighth), still a key commercial corner in College View. The two-story building at center was the Bank of College View from 1906 until the 1920s. It is now part of The Mill coffeehouse. On the horizon at left is a faint view of St. Thomas Orphanage, located two miles away on South Twenty-seventh Street. (JM.)

BISHOP'S RESIDENCE. Thomas Bonacum, Lincoln's Catholic bishop, completed this brick and stone residence east of South Twenty-seventh Street and south of Calvert Street in 1894. In 1901, he announced designs for St. Thomas Orphanage on the west side of Twenty-seventh Street, south of his house. The Bishop Heights residential subdivision was developed beginning in the 1950s on the mansion site, while the orphanage grounds were subdivided for the Bishop Square townhouses in 1974. (JM.)

Ten

Out and Around

Buffalo Motel. Following the paving of Forty-eighth Street north from O Street after World War II, Harvey Gates purchased a tract of several acres on the west side of Forty-eighth Street near R Street and built the 18-unit Buffalo Motel. The motel was increased to 44 units and a small swimming pool was added in the 1950s. The property was purchased in 1982 for the Target store currently on the site. (JM.)

DOMINO'S ITALIAN VILLAGE. Tony Domino first opened his Italian Village in 1936 at Fifty-eighth and O Streets, calling it a "small Dine-Dance place." The original building was destroyed by fire in 1951 and rebuilt as shown. It was sold in 1960 to the Legionnaire Club of Lincoln. A marble fountain of Cupid that was sculpted in 1957 for the restaurant was donated by the club to the Lincoln Parks Department. (EZ.)

LEGIONNAIRE CLUB. In 1960, the Legionnaire Club in the former Domino's Italian Village at O Street and Cotner Boulevard became the 14th location for American Legion Post No. 3, founded in 1919. A second floor was added in 1971 to accommodate the group, which claimed the largest membership among American Legion posts in the early 1990s. The Legionnaire Club moved to smaller quarters at 5630 P Street in 1996 and closed in 2002. (JM.)

FLEETWING SERVICE STATION. The elegant Fleetwing Service Station on the southwest corner of Cotner Boulevard and O Street was designed and built in 1927 by Max William Taylor, a distributor of petroleum products. Taylor's family once owned the section bounded by A, O, Fifty-sixth, and Seventieth Streets, where Taylor Park and Taylor Meadows bear their name. Managed by Elmont S. "Mac" McKee, Fleetwing advertised "courteous, snappy service." (JM.)

GATEWAY SHOPPING CENTER. Bankers' Life Insurance Company moved from downtown Lincoln to new headquarters at Cotner Boulevard and O Streets in the late 1950s. Adjacent to the east, Bankers' Life developed Gateway Shopping Center, which opened in 1960. Landscape architect Larry Halpin of California designed the landscaped mall space shown on this postcard; this was absorbed into the interior of Gateway Mall as the center grew. (JM.)

U.S. VETERANS HOSPITAL. Lincoln's Veterans Hospital opened in 1930, just a year after the Leavitt farm on the south side of O Street was acquired for the hospital grounds. The rural site was described by a Lincoln newspaper as being "four miles east of Lincoln." The principal buildings are arrayed along a curved drive and face a wide lawn. The main hospital, originally topped with a cupola, is centered on the east axis of the state capitol. The entire hospital campus is listed in the National Register of Historic Places. A long-term, phased redevelopment of the campus began in the 2010s, planned with respect for the historic landscape design and buildings. New housing for veterans was built in the northeast corner of the campus in 2017, and a new VA Clinic opened at the north edge in 2021. (Above, EZ; below, JM.)

STAFF RESIDENCES AT U.S. VETERANS HOSPITAL. North of the main hospital, four residential structures were built of brick in the Colonial Revival style seen throughout the campus. This postcard shows the nurses' residence at right and a duplex for physicians' families at left. Located farther along the north curve are another duplex for physicians and a single-family home for a senior physician, as shown in the aerial photograph on the previous page. (EZ.)

LINCOLN PARK THEATRE. Lincoln Park was established in the late 1880s on the southwest corner of First and Van Dorn Streets. It featured a mile-long horse track; roaming buffalo, elk, and other animals; and two restaurants/theaters that entertained as many as 180,000 patrons per year. When 450 incandescent lights and 12 arc lights were installed in 1916, the park's name was changed to Electric Park. The site is now part of Wilderness Park. (EZ.)

EPWORTH PARK. A tract of several hundred acres immediately south of Calvert Street and Lincoln Park was purchased by the Epworth League of the Methodist church in 1896. The doughnut-shaped lake was established surrounding a small island. The main grounds had a 3,000-seat amphitheater, five restaurants, a post office, a hotel, a grocery story, a bakery, and bathhouses. For the Epworth League's 10-day camp meetings, railroads offered fares from Lincoln discounted to half price plus 50¢. The Epworth gatherings became the second-largest religious meetings in the country, overshadowed only by those in Lake Chautauqua, New York. Evening presentations featured speakers like William Jennings Bryan and Booker T. Washington, as well as singer Enrico Caruso and magicians and musicians. (Both, EZ.)

NEBRASKA INSANE ASYLUM. Originally named the State Lunatic Asylum and situated on several hundred acres west of Lincoln and north of the Yankee Hill settlement, the asylum's first frame building burned down in 1871, three months after its completion. Rebuilt with partial funding from insurance, complete with an artesian well in the basement, the four-story stone building is shown here along with several additions. (JM.)

NEBRASKA HOSPITAL FOR THE INSANE, 1940S. The Nebraska Insane Asylum was renamed in the late 1930s to Nebraska Hospital for the Insane. This aerial view looking northwest shows the state hospital when the campus housed well over 1,000 patients. Now known as the Lincoln Regional Center, the 250-bed state psychiatric hospital's 107 acre grounds include a state arboretum with over 400 species of trees and plants. (JM.)

BISON STATUE AT BUFFALO CIRCLE, PIONEERS PARK. John F. Harris, a New York investment banker and former Lincolnite, donated 600 acres to create a large municipal park southwest of Lincoln, which was dedicated as Pioneers Park in 1930. Harris also donated the bronze sculpture of an American bison by French artist George Gardet as the focal point at the park's east entrance. Ernst Herminghaus prepared the park's landscape design. (JM.)

PINEWOOD BOWL. An outdoor amphitheater was included in the earliest plans for Pioneers Park, but construction of the Pinewood Bowl did not begin until 1947, with completion coming in 1951. It is located in a naturally occurring "bowl" surrounded by coniferous plantings to enhance the sense of enclosure. It remains a popular venue for amateur summer musicals and a wide variety of professional touring musicians. (JM.)

THE SMOKE SIGNAL OR CHIEF RED CLOUD. Ellis Luis Burman sculpted this 15-foot-tall figure in "cast stone"—concrete—as a work relief project with multiple federal agencies providing approximately $2,000 for the artwork, landscape improvements, and an elaborate dedication ceremony. The unveiling in 1935 on a hilltop west of the Pinewood Bowl was attended by 100 Native Americans from at least four tribes. Red Cloud, or Mahpiya Luta (1822–1909), was one of the most important political and military leaders of the Oglala Lakota Nation. (JM.)

WESTERN MILITARY ACADEMY. The building shown above opened 2.5 miles southwest of Lincoln as Western Normal Academy in 1891, only to close in the depression of the mid-1890s. It reopened in 1908 as Western Military Academy (for high school boys) under the direction of B.D. Hayward. Within a month, the school burned down. While rebuilding, Hayward temporarily relocated to a former convent near Fifteenth and U Streets. Redesigned by George Berlinghof, Western Military Academy incorporated remnants of walls and the truncated tower of the burned building, with crenelation atop all walls. The school continued from 1909 until Hayward's death in 1916. The State of Nebraska acquired the property on West Van Dorn Street in 1921 for a men's reformatory, shown below. The site across from the north entrance to Pioneers Park still houses a penal facility (in new buildings). (Above, JM; below, EZ.)

CAPITAL BEACH. In 1891, Edward Bignell of the Burlington Railroad dammed Oak Creek to form a 1,000-acre salt lake and Burlington Beach park, then transported the *Belle of the Blue* pleasure boat by flatcar from Crete's Blue River to his lake. Once a viaduct opened across the Lincoln rail yard in 1894, streetcars brought attendees to the amusement park, which was renamed Capital Beach in 1906. It closed in 1961 and was redeveloped with lakeside homes. (JM.)

LINCOLN AIR FORCE BASE. Lincoln became home to one of 11 Army airfields constructed in Nebraska in 1942. Lincoln's airfield reverted to civilian use after World War II. Lincoln Air Force Base (LAFB) was authorized in 1952 during the Cold War, with $29 million spent on new buildings and runways. Thousands of airmen and their families came to Lincoln. When LAFB closed in 1966, Lincoln recouped 2,000 acres and extensive aviation facilities. (JM.)

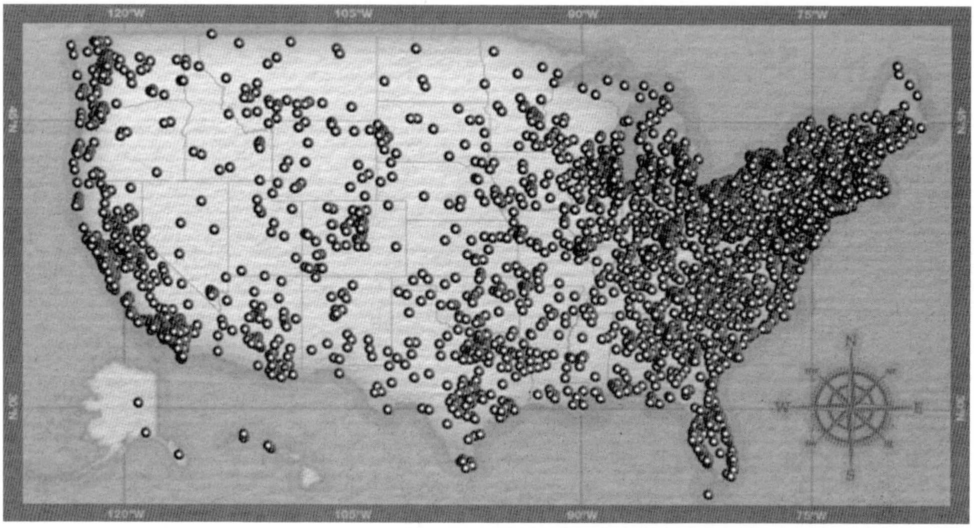